The Toyota Way
in Sales and Marketing

The Toyota Way
in Sales and Marketing

Yoshio Ishizaka

Originally published as *Toyota Hanbai Houshiki* , copyright 2008 by Asa Publishing Co., LTD Publishing Company, Tokyo, Japan.

Address all comments and inquiries to:

Enna Products Corporation
1602 Carolina St.
Unit B3
Bellingham, WA 98229
Telephone: (360) 306-5369
Fax: (905) 481-0756
E-mail: info@enna.com

Printed in the United States of America

Library of Congress Cataloging-in-Publication Data
Ishikaza, Yoshio, 1940,
The Toyota Way in Sales and Marketing
  Includes index.
  ISBN 978-1-926537-08-5
  1. Toyota 2. Sales and Marketing 3. Innovation 4. Management

Written by Yoshio Ishizaka

English translation by Junpei Nakamuro (ENNA)
Edited by Collin McLoughlin (ENNA)

Special thanks to the following people at Toyota Motor Corporation
(TMC), Toyota Motor Sales, U.S.A., Inc. (TMS), Global Knowledge
Center, and Ishida Taiseisha Inc. (ITP) for their help and support:

John Kramer (TMS-GKC)
Rick Taniguchi (TMC-GKC)
Masuaki Koizumi (TMC-GKC)
Hiroyuki Yasuma (ITP)
Shinichi Kobayashi (ITP)

Table of Contents

CHAPTER 1

CHAPTER 2

CHAPTER 3

CHAPTER 4

CHAPTER 5

CHAPTER 6

CHAPTER 7

FOREWORD

When I wrote *The Toyota Way* in 2004 one of my inspirations was an internal Toyota document called *The Toyota Way 2001*. It was more of a long booklet than a book, but like many Toyota documents it was short, concise, and full of wisdom. The book was organized around a simple model with two pillars — respect for people and continuous improvement. Continuous improvement is what makes the business strong at Toyota. Many people assume it means that Toyota wants only small, incremental changes, but that is a misunderstanding. What it really means is that Toyota wants improvements, big and small, continuously. Many companies make big improvements from time to time but then after the big change things settle back to normal. What that looks like in practice is a big cost reduction and then no improvement, so costs creep back up—or perhaps it is a big improvement in quality through a quality program and then people lose focus and quality sneaks back down. Toyota's view is that without continuous improvement big changes will make the company's progress look like the business cycle, up and down and up and down. That does not satisfy a company with high aspirations like Toyota. At Toyota they expect continual upward progress. Even in a business downturn, like the 2008-2009 shock that dragged sales down by one-third, Toyota wants improvement. Obviously they cannot improve sales when customers are not buying, but they can improve quality, reduce cost, and develop the capabilities of team members in continuous improvement.

Why should team members contribute to continuous improvement? In many companies it would be for the privilege of losing their jobs at the first sign of reduced quarterly profits. At Toyota they have the simple belief that if you want the team member to commit to the company the company must commit to the team member. That is respect for people. The company cannot commit 100 percent to lifetime employment and promise they will let the company go out of business before any team member loses their job, but they can commit that layoffs will be the last drastic step after all other possibilities are exhausted. Nor is the loss of money for a few quarters sufficient reason for layoffs. The only good reason is an actual threat to solvency— they are running out of cash. Since the company hoards cash in profitable times that is not likely.

It was several years later that I realized that another document was written to accompany *The Toyota Way 2001*, which is the basis for the book you have before you. It was called *The Toyota Way in Sales and Marketing* and the writing was led by

Yoshio Ishizaka. Toyota is a manufacturing company first and Ishizaka-san believed there was a document that needed to speak clearly to the special role of Toyota Motor Sales in the company. The core values of the company were its core values and that does not change whether it is engineering or manufacturing or sales, so there is a lot of overlap in the documents. There are also distinctive elements that the sales organization can better understand.

Principles like genchi-genbutsu are the same wherever you are in the company. In a factory you might go to the assembly line to observe production and look for waste to eliminate. In sales you must go to where the customer is to understand how they use the product and what their concerns are about their cars and customer service.

There are many famous stories in Toyota Motor Sales about working with the chief engineers. At Toyota there is an unusual system that gives the chief engineer extraordinary power over the design and engineering of a vehicle. "It is the chief engineer's car" people will say. Ask an engineer working on a development program how they know what the customer wants and they are likely to say we listen to the chief engineer. Ask someone in marketing how they influence the design of the vehicle and they say we must convince the chief engineer. With that much responsibility the chief engineer must have a lot of data, but also a lot of intuition about what customers want. They get that informed intuition through genchi-genbutsu — they go and see first hand.

The Chief Engineer of the Sienna minivan did this by driving through every state in the United State and every part of Canada and Mexico — personally. Chief engineers for Scion have gone to many youth-oriented activities sponsored by Scion. A chief engineer for a Lexus model arranged to live for a week with a rich American family. The stories go on and on but they speak to the importance of direct contact and observation.

Direct contact also means establishing relationships. Throughout Toyota relationships mean a great deal. In the heart of the recession Toyota executives from Japan seemed to be everyplace in the United States, checking on morale, checking on the dealers, checking on the customers. Akio Toyoda made a surprise visit to my town of Ann Arbor, Michigan to visit a local Toyota dealership. This is very unusual in the United States, but very natural in Toyota. You go and see to really understand the actual situation, but also to establish relationships. Toyota speaks of establishing relationships with customers for life. They do not simply mean customers should buy their cars, but there should be a connection between the customers and the company.

Putting customers first is more than a slogan at Toyota. They work hard to ingrain in every engineer, every person in the sales organization, and every person building cars that the company exists to serve customers and society. If Toyota designs and builds quality cars that are what customers want and sells them at market cost, the company will prosper and all team members and partners will prosper. It is never acceptable to sacrifice quality or customer service for the sake of short-term costs.

This book expands on and explains the internal Toyota document on sales and marketing in a way that should speak to all those in sales organizations throughout the world. It offers deep insights into Toyota's way of thinking. In most cases Toyota keeps internal documents internal. They may leak out but they are not actively promoted by Toyota. This book is a rare instance in which Toyota gave its blessing and decided to share their view of continuous improvement in sales and customer service. It is a gift and I sincerely recommend that you read it, learn from it, and enjoy it.

Jeffrey K. Liker

Professor, University of Michigan

Author's Message

Toyota Motor Corporation celebrated its 70th Anniversary in 2007 and became the top auto manufacturer in the world after having produced approximately 9.5 million cars worldwide on a consolidated basis and exceeded the production volume of its closest competitor, General Motors of America. In the last decade, Toyota's production volume has increased exponentially. As a matter of fact, as I move my pen writing this very book, Toyota cars are being assembled at a surprising rate of 1 car every 3 seconds in 53 factories located in 27 different countries worldwide. Toyota no longer limits their marketing operations to Japanese customers and has gone beyond the basic domestic framework in order to become a successful global corporation. Of these finished cars, 72 percent are being marketed and sold in about 170 countries with the United States of America being the most prominent country where Toyota cars are being sold. This means that there are more countries where Toyota cars can be found than either McDonald's or Starbucks. It is safe to say that Toyota now recognizes Japan as merely a part of their global marketing territory.

As I dedicated myself to Toyota for more than 40 years, I have various emotions about Toyota's tremendous success. Half of the time, I am extremely honored to have been part of Toyota's achievement; at the same time, I feel as if I am merely dreaming about the whole thing. During this time period, many changes have taken place and some things have remained the same. I admit that Toyota could be called an old-fashioned company. The organization has been anchored on the same principles and values over the years which have proved to be a major competitive advantage. The conundrum has been to be flexible in the face of global change and the expansion in various markets while maintaining its core values.

People often ask me what made Toyota the most successful company in the world. With such a question, I do not think it is acceptable to answer by either simply describing newly-formed principles, or some fancy English terms which many people speak about nowadays. This is because I strongly believe that Toyota's success is merely a result of legitimate practices of genchi-genbutsu (the actual item in the actual place), prioritizing valuable customers, assembling better quality cars, and simply providing flawless services on a daily basis, since the very beginning. I may not be the best person to answer this question, but who can really establish cause and effect? One can only recap the events and principles that were at play in achieving the results. I decided to write this book as there have been almost no well-organized books published on the topic of the sales and marketing aspects of Toyota.

When people mention Toyota, the Toyota Production System is always discussed and emphasized. Even though I understand that I am no expert in the Toyota Production System, I truly appreciate the knowledge and techniques formulated by Mr. Taiichi Ohno and many other innovators in the past, which have built a strong foundation for Toyota's production management systems.

Another key distinction has been the holistic approach of the organization. Production and sales are essentially indispensable to each other. The main reason for Toyota's success is that their production and sales operation have been fused together in the most functional manner. The integration of market research, product design, development, engineering, manufacturing, and marketing is indicative of Toyota's synergistic approach.

Toyota's achievement in competing on a global scale cannot be fully explained without analyzing their sales and marketing way. In 2002, I started putting together a report entitled "The Toyota Way in Sales and Marketing" (TWSM). My initial intention was to create a document that would facilitate the understanding of the "All Toyota" mentality to accommodate the rapid expansion of globalization at the time.

Since I joined Toyota, I have been engaged in nothing but sales and marketing activities on the front line. In Australia, I learned the fundamentals of what it takes to succeed in a foreign culture. In America, I held an important responsibility in launching the Lexus brand and I subsequently had the honor of serving Toyota Motor Sales, U.S.A., Inc. (TMS, U.S.A.) as president of the company. I was reassigned to the position of Executive Vice President of Toyota Motor Corporation in Japan in 2001. Judging from these various leadership responsibilities in my career, I feel an obligation to write about the Toyota Way in Sales and Marketing. The fundamental questions this book answers are:

What is the Toyota Way in Sales and Marketing that helped establish Toyota to be the best?

What are the fundamental differences between Toyota's marketing and production methods?

By describing the Toyota Way in terms of sales and marketing and providing insights about Toyota as an organization and the philosophy that is built into their daily mind set, I am honored to help, in anyway, those who are striving to be successful in this competitive global market.

Yoshio Ishizaka

Mr. Yoshio Ishizaka

CHAPTER 1

SALES AND MARKETING METHODS TO BE LEARNED FROM THE WORLD

Assuring a Common Mindset — How Toyota Employs more than 200,000

In order to understand Toyota's sales and marketing approach, I first need to explain the "Toyota Way." In April of 2001, Toyota formulated *The Toyota Way 2001*, a document that clearly states Toyota's unique management culture, value system, and the inherent philosophy contained in operation manuals, so that specific goals can always be achieved. It is written based upon two imperatives, *Intelligence* and *Kaizen*, which are also referred to as *Respect for People* , and *Continuous Improvements*.

1

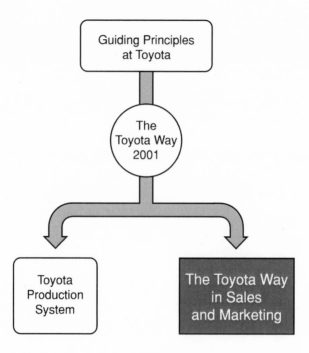

Figure 1: Guiding Principles of Toyota

Each chapter teaches workers the fundamental rules in terms of 5 key concepts such as, *Challenge, Kaizen, Genchigenbutsu, Respect,* and *Teamwork*. Even before *The Toyota Way 2001* was written and made available for dissemination, these principles were always kept in our minds as something to be shared among Toyota workers. This mindset has become part of employees' identity and part of Toyota's signature practices. In reality these principles are being taught by senior workers to new workers through their words and behaviors as if they were implicit common knowledge on the shop floor. The result is both experiential and conceptual. Employees learn the Toyota Way and experience what it means from their first day in the company and throughout their career at Toyota.

Why did this implicit knowledge have to be written out for sharing?

Toyota has grown too large to depend solely upon traditional verbal transmission of knowledge and unspoken standards that are conveyed to workers. With large-scale worldwide operations and more than some 200,000 employees, it is crucial and inevitable that these principles be clearly written out and published to reach a wider global audience. With different languages, customs, and environments unique to each region, *The Toyota Way 2001* had to be published in a clear and organized manner. Experience has also shown these principles to be independent of culture or language and form the ethos of being a Toyota employee.

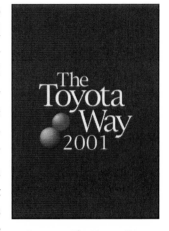

Figure 2: The Toyota Way 2001

©Toyota Motor Corporation
Used with permission. Permission does not imply endorsement.

This book, *The Toyota Way in Sales and Marketing*, will show how the Toyota spirit and know-how related to sales and marketing has its roots in *The Toyota Way 2001*.

Toyota's Implicit Knowledge was Put in Statutory Form in 2001

As mentioned in the previous section, I need to explain further how *The Toyota Way 2001* forms the foundation of this book. *Intelligence and Kaizen,* and *Respect for People,* are the two pillars on which the Toyota Way rests. *Intelligence and Kaizen* describes an attitude in which you are never satisfied

2 Pillars of the Toyota Way

Challenge

Kaizen
(Continuous improvement)

Genchi Genbutsu

Respect

Teamwork

Kaizen and Intelligence

Respect for People

Figure 3: The Two Pillars

with the current condition and continuously develop innovative ideas yielding higher added-values. On the other hand, *Respect*

3

for People takes into consideration and pays regard to five stakeholders such as customers, dealers, employees, suppliers, local society, and shareholders. Toyota and many other organizations realize that the starting point and key building block is the employees. The development of each worker can be directly related with performance. Each group is affected by the performance of the company.

Every Toyota employee is expected to keep these two concepts in mind at all times and base their actions on these principles. Additionally, these two concepts can be further described by 5 key words. *Intelligence and Kaizen* can be broken into "Challenge," "Kaizen," and "Genchi-genbutsu." *Respect for People* is composed of "Respect" and "Teamwork." These five building blocks help you gain a clearer grasp of the meaning of each individual pillar.

Figure 4: Ingredients to Intelligence and Kaizen

1. Challenge

The first keyword *Challenge* guides us to setting higher objectives for achieving an ideal condition and continuously realizing such goals with courage and creativity. In other words, this implies the innate spirit of Toyota is to continuously pursue the creation of value-adding activities, which is the core of Toyota's fundamental obligation to the society; what we call the "Art of Manufacturing." Any challenge always comes with risk. However, *Challenge* as described here allows you to try the best you can as long as your goals are based on well-established and sound principles. Part of the challenge is to stay competitive by moving forward at all times, thus challenging the status quo is a necessity. This implies venturing into new and sometimes difficult areas while staying true to the Toyota Way.

2. Continuous Improvement, Kaizen

Kaizen has become a self-explanatory term among those companies that research Toyota nowadays. I suspect that most people think of this term when they think about the Toyota Way. At Toyota, where both evolution and revolution are continuously pursued and their efforts toward improvement are never-ending, Toyota possesses a unique corporate culture summarized by Mr. Hiroshi Okuda, the former chairman of Toyota as, "the worst thing to do is to change nothing." This implies that we should not simply give up our efforts based upon unfavorable experiences of the past, taboos, or simply judging that something is simply impossible to overcome. Instead we should utilize our creativity to the fullest extent in order to make sure that our problems can be solved.

When I visited a factory for inspection, I was often surprised to see significant changes had been brought into a certain process. For instance, I had the following dialog with shop floor workers in the past. I asked, "What did you do to make this process perform so differently now? It is nothing like six months ago."

A worker replied, "We have found a better way to perform the process. We continuously improved it to make everything easier."

Kaizen should not be forced by instructions from superiors. *Kaizen* must be pro–actively initiated by workers who seek solutions while analyzing structural problems. This requires each shop floor worker to acknowledge the current condition and learn from mistakes in order to prevent the same errors. After such *Kaizen* practices are firmly set in place, the proven way of conducting a certain process must be standardized and implemented throughout the organization. It is also important to practice *Kaizen* endlessly on a daily basis. *Constant, Consistent, and Continuous Kaizen* is simply a daily activity in Toyota. This is called the "3C" philosophy.

3. Genchi-genbutsu

Production System and Lean Production

Kaizen requires comprehensive understanding of a current condition and discovery of the true cause of problems before formulating solutions. What becomes important in this respect is the third keyword *genchi-genbutsu*. *Genchi-genbutsu* allows us to analyze the nature of a given condition, establish consensus, make sound decisions, and attack problems with our full efforts. This attitude remains the most fundamental mindset among Toyota workers. My predecessors used to tell me, "Go see the Genba (on the floor) first," and "Do not make your decision before you analyze the actual item." I also made a habit of saying the same to my subordinates over the years. I admit that Toyota has had a tendency for running into—what seems to be—daydreaming discussions while intentionally spending a large amount of time debating strategies and some trivial arguments. However, this is evidence of Toyota's corporate culture built upon the traditional *genchi-genbutsu* principle.

Respect For People

The three principles I have described so far, *Challenge*, *Kaizen*, and *Genchi-genbutsu* are essential ingredients in the first pillar concept, *Intelligence and Kaizen*. In contrast, the forth keyword, *Respect*, and the fifth keyword, *Teamwork* are strongly tied with *Respect for People*, that is found in the second pillar concept.

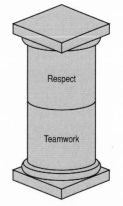

Figure 5: Ingredients to Respect for People

1. Respect

Respect means paying your highest regards to other people, establishing mutual understandings in the most sincere manner, and everyone fulfilling their responsibilities. As the first president of the Toyota Motors Sales (Hanbai), Mr. Shotaro Kamiya

said, "Customers come first, then dealers, and finally the manufacturer comes last." It is always in Toyota's awareness that sincere mutual understandings and an explanation of their role in
society must be provided to all of their stakeholders, including
customers as well as corporate clients.

2. Teamwork

Needless to say, Toyota employees are treated in the same manner. Toyota believes that respect among their employees can be
established by creating opportunities for carrying out open and
fair discussions at any given time. This treatment also leads employees to become loyal to their company and understand the
significance of *Teamwork*. The Japanese have a strong culture of
collective effort toward achieving a unified goal. Toyota's true
strength here is that they can translate this unique culture into
a universal language that every ordinary person around the
world can understand as a simple joy of accomplishing something as a human being. Continue your work while caring for
others. Instead of being self-centered, both on a personal and
corporate level, Toyota emphasizes training of their employees
and tapping each employee's ability to the fullest in the hope
that the company can grow with their valuable employees as
well as other corporate clients. This is what Toyota really means
by teamwork.

At different times in history, organizations gained promi-
nence through innovation. The automobile industry began in
1886 by German engineer Carl Benz. He opened a curtain to the
automobile world by inventing the first practical car running
with a gasoline fuel mechanism. After that, it was Henry Ford
who succeeded in making this technology widely available to
the public.

Ford established a manufacturing system in the early 20th
century in which production cost was significantly minimized
by a mass production system with built-in flow operations. By

this, Ford was able to maintain affordable automobile cost that eventually led to the creation of an "Automobile Society." Consequently, Ford's mass production system was introduced not only to the automotive industry, but was also widely spread among many other prominent 20th century industrial organizations. General Motors followed by focusing on customers' tastes by offering choices of color. Toyota applied these production systems accordingly as a starting point of their operations. However, what has been so different about Toyota is that they have conducted kaizen based on the "3C" philosophy, which in turn gave birth to a whole new manufacturing mechanism.

I intend to describe details of the Toyota Production System in later chapters. In summary, the Toyota Production System aims at reducing production cost and achieving absolute elimination of wastes by supplying components and finished products, Just-In-Time. In the year 1980, the Massachusetts Institute of Technology (MIT located in the US) spent a tremendous amount of money in conducting a research project in order to unveil the mechanism of the Toyota Production System. The results of this research was published in a systematic manner in a book titled *The Machine That Changed the World*. The book clearly stated that the Toyota Production System had gone beyond a mass production system and should be referred to as a "Lean Production System." What does the word, "Lean" imply here? It describes a production system that is physically fit without any excessive body fat, so to speak. As the research revealed, Lean production

Figure 6: *The Machine That Changed the World*

has been known as the core of the Toyota Way. However, one thing we cannot forget here is that it is simply a result of applying endless kaizen efforts to Ford's mass production system and a focus on the changing needs of customers.

History of Separation between Production and Sales

Toyota Motor Co., Ltd. was founded in 1937. After World War II, in 1950, it was faced with a severe management crisis. During the economic recession, Toyota managed to overcome this crisis by receiving emergency financial assistance from their bank. Under strict conditions the sales department and the production departments were set up as individual entities. That is how Toyota Motor Sales Co., Ltd. was initiated. For more than 20 years, production and sales activities were conducted independently of one another. Finally, in 1982, Toyota became what it is today after sales and production divisions were amalgamated.

Upon graduation from university in 1964, I was employed at the sales division. This was right in the middle of the separation period between sales and production. The separation did not mean that the departments did not get along with one another. On the contrary, I admit that separation was the best thing to happen so that each division could fulfill its own objectives as well as inspiring the other to higher achievement.

Figure 7: The Author and his wife, 1964

In 1964 when the Olympics took place in Tokyo, color televisions rapidly became a popular item in households. Through this media, various corporate images and marketing strategies were broadcast to consumers. There was one catch phrase that was quoted more than others: "Toyota is all about Sales and Services, Nissan is all about Technology and Exporting." The phrases accurately described the competitive characteristics of each corporation. As a matter of fact, at that time, Toyota had a strong sales record in the domestic market due to a strong network of dealers that had been built up since the beginning of Toyota. However, Nissan was clearly ahead of Toyota in terms of the volume of exported products to foreign countries.

Before I started my career I told myself, "Japanese cars will become even more in demand overseas, and the volume of export is going to increase to accommodate that increased demand." Every time I came across the catch phrase "Nissan is all about Exporting," I made a strong commitment and awoke my fighting spirit against Nissan to help Toyota overturn this image. At the same time, I felt even more proud of our catch phrase "Toyota is all about Sales." Even though Toyota was separated into sales and production at the time, the company possessed a true competitive spirit. Needless to say, this same competitive spirit still thrives in Toyota today.

Is the Toyota Way Limited only to Production?

When I go to bookstores in search of books written about Toyota, I always discover one shelf after another of books that focus merely on the Toyota Production System. I strongly suspect that the general public equates the Toyota Way to the Toyota Production System. This perception is an oversimplification that is in no way close to reality.

Just as the production division has their own Toyota Way, the sales department also applies their own version of the Toyota Way. The same is true with other functions such as human resources, accounting, and supply-chain management. Each function has its own unique and customized version of the Toyota Way in order to achieve higher levels of productivity.

As far as the sales division is concerned, they have often thought about publishing *The Toyota Way in Sales and Marketing* in the past. However, their effort has never been realized until now. Conducting sales not only includes managing systems and techniques, but also must take into consideration human networking and valuable communications that cannot be easily systematized or standardized. This is what has made the publication of *The Toyota Way in Sales and Marketing* extremely challenging as no single book has been available to us on this matter.

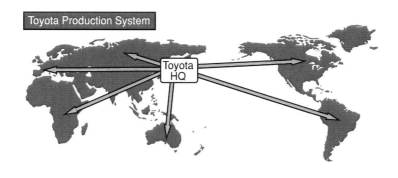

Figure 8: Toyota Production System Implementation

Most of you already know that the Toyota Production System gave birth to Lean Production, which is strongly supported by "Just-In-Time" and "Jidoka." Just-In-Time is a method for producing the needed items and components in the needed quantity only at the time needed. Jidoka is a philosophy that integrates human intelligence with machinery. It also allows each worker to stop the entire production line in order to eliminate defects immediately upon discovering any abnormalities or mistakes on the shop floor. Jidoka does not just mean automated processes; it must be clearly separated from it and referred to as "Automation with a Human Touch." Various techniques such as "Standardized Work" and "Small-lot Production," with the integration of unique tools such as "Kanbans" and "Andon Lights" are being used for the purpose of crystallizing "Just-In-Time" and "Jidoka" into reality.

The Toyota Production System has been able to attract much attention because such techniques and tools have shown to be easily applicable to every day operation in many other companies, in any number of industries, worldwide. So, my question is:

Is it possible to expect the same reaction for the Toyota Way in Sales and Marketing?

Undoubtedly yes, it is possible. Toyota sales operations indeed have their own innovations, tools, and built-in systems to put into practice the Toyota Way. Toyota's guidance on networking and communication must be appealing to any company or business leader, especially in present times when our conception of what it means to be a good company changes drastically.

Figure 9: 9th Toyota President, Mr. Fujio Cho

The global competitive environment and the speed of change favors the fittest. Toyota as a whole, has wanted to clearly state the definition of their sales and marketing principles. Mr. Fujio Cho, the president at the time, wrote in the beginning of *The Toyota Way 2001* bulletin:

"I believe that the Toyota Way continues to evolve itself towards the future as our unspoken management principles and techniques in every single division within the company become written policies for everyone to share."

Mechanism for Collecting Knowledge and Know-how from Around the World

As it was my strong desire to define the application of the Toyota Way in conducting sales, I spent about one year compiling a small 70-page bulletin titled *The Toyota Way in Sales and Marketing*. Because the color of the book cover is silver, it is often referred to as the "Silver Book." It was first written in both Japanese and English, and has since been translated into numerous other languages, including Spanish and Arabic. It was destined to become extremely valuable information to other Toyota workers involved in sales activities. I wrote this "Silver Book" while in the role of Executive Vice-President.

I established a small study team involving Mr. Isao Endo (Professor, Waseda University Graduate School), Mr. Yukitoshi Funo (current Chairman of Toyota Motor Sales, U.S.A., Inc.) and Mr. Katsuyoshi Tabata (General Manager of Toyota's Global Marketing Department at the time) and organized a brainstorming session with them. I asked Professor Endo how other prominent global organizations such as McDonald's, Walt Disney, and CitiBank, respectively, had been able to consolidate their own unique philosophy into an organized fashion.

From the start, one thing that helped us to effectively articulate a definition of the Toyota Way in Sales and Marketing, was the idea that good techniques and concepts from around the world ought to be collected first, and that it be based upon careful, factual observation. This seemed to be, in my opinion, a much more honest and objective approach than how the Toyota Production System is generally expounded upon in the popular press. The initial effort with the Toyota Production System took the approach of going outward from "Japan to the World." Doing so limited the available background information of successful examples available only in Japan, meaning that systems and techniques originating from Japanese factories were transplanted into factories located overseas.

13

On the other hand, the Toyota Way in Sales and Marketing system integrated empirical data collected from Toyota operations from around the world. They created the opportunity for such information to be disseminated, evaluated, and assessed by those who read it. It truly is "global benchmarking of critical information."

Toyota Marketing= Global Benchmarking

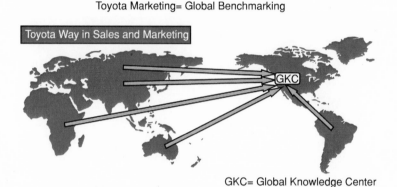

GKC= Global Knowledge Center

Figure 10: Toyota Marketing System Implementation

Systems and techniques associated with sales and marketing vary significantly depending upon the environment or customs of a country or region. For example, when we compare Japanese and US retail stores, we find completely different management practices. Therefore, implementing Japanese sales practices and techniques directly to overseas markets without localizing the content simply will not work. It is not an over-exaggeration to say that, when studying ten different countries, ten different customs and professional environments can be identified.

In order to define Toyota's marketing system to be shared among all of us, it is extremely important to collect and translate successful stories from around the world into key principles that are truly applicable to every country's unique situation.

Knowledge Sharing through the Global Knowledge Center

The Silver Book was completed in the fall of 2001 and was distributed among all Toyota employees working in sales and customer support departments, worldwide. As I will explain the content of the Silver Book in Chapter 2, I am proud to present it as the bible for conveying the philosophy upon which

Figure II: Global Knowledge Center

©Toyota Motor Corporation
Used with permission. Permission does not imply endorsement.

the Toyota Way in Sales and Marketing is based. However, we knew that our mission did not end here. It did not mean anything unless our philosophy became an asset to the shop floor and was actually implemented into real situations, worldwide.

How do we apply the philosophy to our daily activities?

In order to disseminate the ideas from the Silver Book to Toyota employees in the most manageable fashion, yet still remain fully detailed, we decided to create an information outlet for transferring the knowledge. In order to fulfill this purpose, in July of 2002, the Global Knowledge Center (GKC) was established at the University of Toyota located at Toyota Motor Sales, U.S.A., Inc. This strategy was not unlike the practice of many U.S. corporations such as Motorola or McDonald's.

The main objective of GKC is to welcome Toyota executives from all over the world to participate in open discussions. The topics focused on the direction the Silver Book ought to take in order to spread its findings across the world. In this context, successful stories from every part of the marketing territories are most likely be reported and discussed. To take full advantage of this opportunity, a new company bulletin called the "Best Practice Bulletin" was created and distributed regularly so that the information could be shared with a much larger audience.

By combining three types of such medias: "Silver Book," "GKC" and "Best Practice Bulletin," The Toyota Way in Sales and Marketing has been successfully adapted with involvement of many Toyota operations around the world as a "Global Benchmarking" effort. In other words, the Toyota Way in Sales and Marketing inspires Toyota employees. It also defines its world-class philosophy and techniques in an organized manner that is essential to guarantee the survival of such a large global corporation as Toyota.

CHAPTER 2

WISDOM OF MARKETING:
THE "SILVER BOOK"

5Ps in Toyota's Marketing System

In this chapter I will outline the five chapters of the Silver Book.
The Silver Book summarizes the philosophy behind the Toyota Marketing System and consists of five important concepts,
known as the 5Ps inside Toyota.

Purpose

The Silver Book is divided into five chapters. In the first chapter, Purpose, we discover that the foundation of the Toyota Production Sys-

tem is based on the accumulated knowledge of our predecessors.

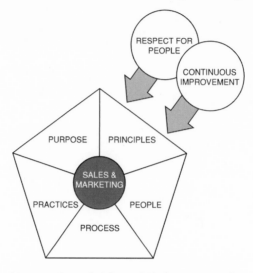

Figure 12: Toyota's Sales and Marketing Principles

Figure 13: Toyota's Collective Mindset

Unity among dealers, worldwide distributors, and Toyota itself is being continuously improved and evolves in order to achieve Toyota's collective mindset. Needless to say, those who are sustaining sales and marketing efforts on the frontline are the retailers and distributors who provide our finished products.

The success of our global marketing strategy is directly linked to the solid relationship of trust between Toyota and such retailers and distributors. With such trust and respect amongst various sectors and a willingness to grow hand–in–hand, Toyota defines Purpose.

People

The chapter entitled People, summarizes Toyota's commitment to "Placing High Value on Human Intelligence." This philosophy takes form with "3Cs for Harmonious Growth," "3Cs for Innovation," and "Just-In-Time" by introducing the powerful lessons from Toyota pioneers such as Messr. Kiichiro Toyoda, Eiji Toyoda, Shoichiro Toyoda, Shotaro Kamiya, Seishi Kato and Taiichi Ohno.

Figure 14: Taiichi Ohno, TPS Creator

©Toyota Motor Corporation. Used with permission. Permission does not imply endorsement.

"3Cs for Harmonious Growth" consists of *Communication, Consideration*, and *Cooperation*. It essentially means that there must be mutual understanding with respect towards others. No actions can be taken unless everyone is fully informed and persuaded for the implementation of the decisions to be successfully carried out.

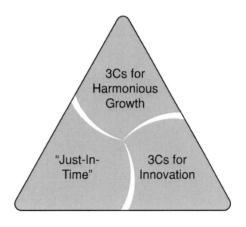

Figure 15: Focus on Placing High Value on Human Intelligence

"3Cs for Innovation" consists of *Creativity, Challenge*, and *Courage*. Toyota has a unique corporate spirit to challenge the impossible and overcome it by continuously battling difficulties and utilizing creativity to the fullest. Without this innate spirit, Toyota would have never been able to become the number one automaker in terms of the volume of production.

Last but not least, "Just-In-Time" is the fundamental principle found in the Toyota Production System for supplying only the necessary items at the necessary time in precise quantities. This principle is also deeply reflected in Toyota's marketing system. We have made a commitment to provide only the necessary volume of essential products, components, and information when needed by our customers across the world.

Figure 16: Toyota's Corporate Vision

Principles

The third P, Principles, indicates the never-changing corporate ideals and vision that will be carried on by following generations of Toyota employees. There are two corporate visions. One is to provide superior products and services to the community, the second is to become the "most successful and respected corporation" in each country where Toyota operates. Toyota calls this unified vision a "Radar for All of Toyota"

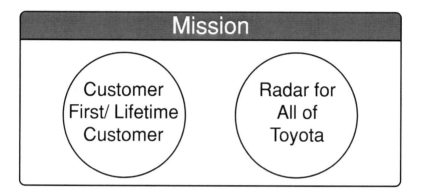

Figure 17: Toyota's Two Corporate Missions

The goal of our work is not to become the number one automaker by selling the highest volume of cars in a reckless manner. Neither is it in Toyota's interest to pump up our stocks to inflate the actual value of our company, nor to acquire other companies — one after another — regardless of what industry they might be in.

Do you agree that any corporation ought to be respected by local people?

Corporations should fully understand the unique culture, customs, environment, and national identity of the host country and provide the best goods and services that improve the lives of local people. I cannot stress enough that the true meaning of "Success" in corporations is to be loved by the people.

Then what is considered to be the best goods and services that Toyota can provide as an automobile company?

The answer to this question is described by the other vision of Toyota, which is "to provide customers with the unparalleled experiences of purchasing and ownership of Toyota cars."

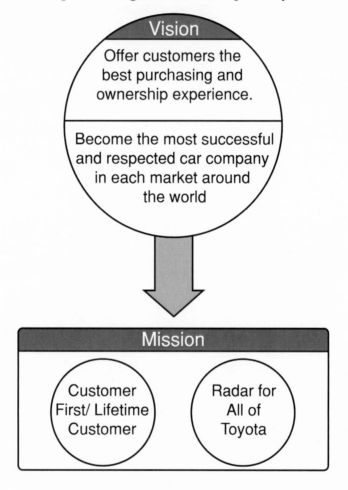

Figure 18: Never Changing Corporate Ideals & Principles

By providing superior customer support and high quality products, customers become fully satisfied with having bought Toyota cars and hold strong desires to continue purchasing Toyota products in the future. This is Toyota's second corporate vision of attracting and retaining customers for life.

Consequently, clear corporate tenets are needed to realize these two significant visions. We have defined two corporate missions; "Customers Come First" and "Radar for All of Toyota." Such marketing spirit to "respond to customer's need in a detailed and thorough manner" is a Toyota tradition that goes back to the beginning of the company. Such a culture must never be forgotten in the rapidly changing environment of each country. These two visions can be realized by firmly complying with these missions and result in "Life-Time Customers." In other words, those who continue to drive Toyota cars can be retained as loyal customers.

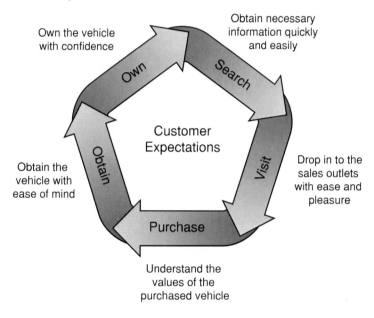

Figure 19: Customer For Life

In addition, marketing departments that deal with customers on the frontline must act as an antenna in order to fulfill the mission. "Radar for All of Toyota" plays an extremely important role in reflecting customer and market demands into policy making. They must act as a critical bridge, establishing an effective two-way communication channel between the company and customers as well as between corporate divisions such as purchasing, development and production departments, and customers.

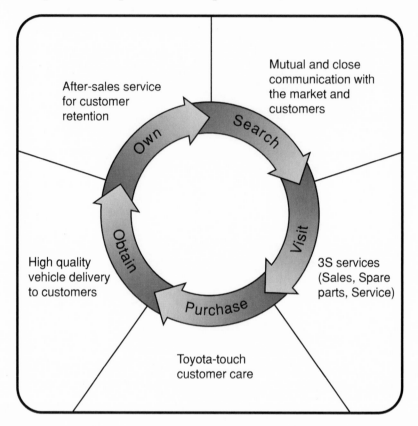

Figure 20: Five Processes

Process

Identifying an appropriate process for achieving visions becomes extremely important when carrying out our missions. The chapter on *Process* describes that in great detail. Toyota is very meticulous about any particular process they implement in order to obtain desired results. Toyota employees constantly ask themselves, "What process should be taken to accomplish this goal?," and "For what reason do we want to meet this goal?"

Such a Process-Oriented mind, so to speak, is built into the DNA of Toyota. For example, how to satisfy and keep customers,

"Customer For Life " as we call it, is arrived at by analyzing what our process of marketing ought to be. Most importantly, a process needs to be formulated by analyzing the customer's point of view.

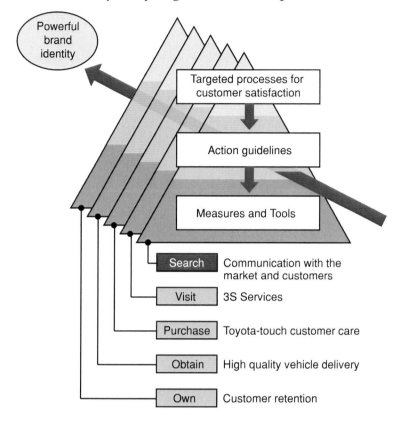

Figure 2I: Powerful Brand Identity

A customer's purchasing process can be divided into the following 5 steps: Search, Visit, Purchase, Obtain, and Own. When a customer purchases a car, they either go online or refer to some magazines to decide what kind of a car he/she would like to own (Search). Then, if he/she becomes interested in Toyota cars, the potential customer comes to a Toyota dealership (Visit) where our cars can be seen and test driven. This is when and where the point of serious discussions about the price and financing (Purchase) takes place. Shortly after purchasing, the brand new car is delivered to the new owner's house (Obtain) and it becomes his/her possession (Own). At any time in this whole process the level of our customer's satisfaction must be high. Each step of the process has its own processes, and must meet its own objectives.

For example:

> Search—The necessary information can be easily and accurately acquired.

> Visit—Customers can visit a retail location with ease and fun.

> Purchase—Customers are given all the options and given the opportunity to be fully convinced with their own decision.

> Obtain—Customers can take ownership of their new car with no stress.

> Own—Customers can enjoy the vehicle without having to worry about anything.

By taking into consideration the customer's point of view and defining what each process ought to be, we defined important objectives for each individual process.

Five Processes Cherished By Toyota's Sales & Marketing

The first process, "Search", is to establish and sustain two-way communications between individual customers and the market. When a customer begins to research our products, it tends to be a one-way communication of information. In such a case, we need to become creative so that two-way communication channels can be established at all times. Toyota must work closely with dealers and distributors in order to effectively convey our message to customers and also collect customer requests and comments so that products can reflect the market demand as much as possible, in a timely manner. Such two-way communications can ensure interest and motivate customer to come into Toyota's retail stores to try out our products first.

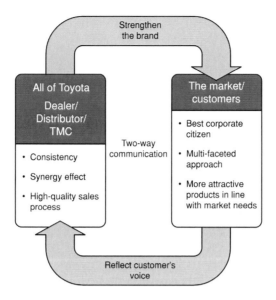

Figure 22: The Search Process

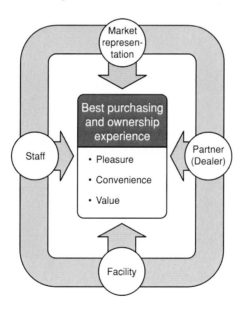

Figure 23: The Visit Process

To support this activity of "Visit," Toyota targets "Integrated 3S Services" (3S) by emphasizing the significance of *Sales, Spare parts*, and *Service* designed to provide customers reassurance in choosing a certain Toyota retail store. We convince our customers that our relationship is far from being over once they purchase our cars. Instead, we guarantee them with after-sales services, such as repairs and maintenance, even before they make the decision to buy.

The most critical part of this process is to initiate direct communications with customers. In order to deepen such relationships between customers and retail stores, each retail store must function based upon "Pleasure," "Convenience," and "Value." Sales staffs in dealerships that operate on the frontline play extremely important roles. Therefore, training of sales associates who can entertain various challenges and win the hearts of customers by conveying to them the true value of Toyota cars becomes absolutely necessary.

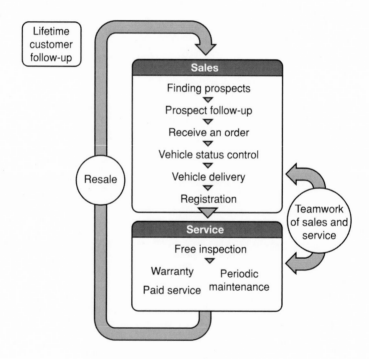

Figure 24: The Purchase Process

The process of "Purchase" requires a flexible approach to customers and must create meaningful and customized contact points with each individual customer. By doing so, our products can be purchased with a great deal of confidence and certitude on the part of the customers. To achieve that, the critical information needs to be shared among every department in Toyota (All Toyota) in a way that can be easily conveyed. Our commitment, "High-quality Lifetime Follow-up for Customers" is the key to the process of "Purchase."

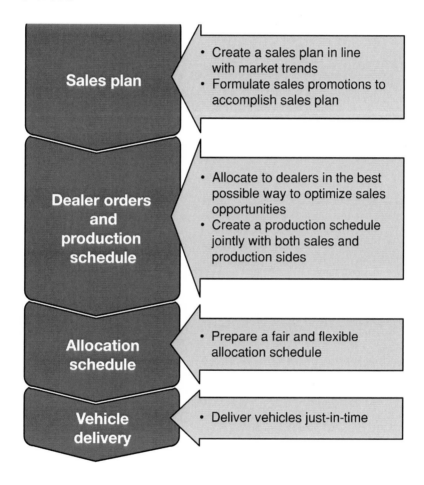

Figure 25: The Obtain Process

Our fourth process, "Obtain" aspires to "Provide Toyota Value" to our customers. This means that customers who just purchased a Toyota car can feel a great deal of satisfaction upon receiving the delivery with a high level of expectation towards their future lives with our products. Supply and demand operations, which focus on both a high rate of inventory turnover and maximum efficiency, are known to be the competitive edge of Toyota. Additional Toyota value can be earned on top of the value of our cars by eliminating any stress imposed on customers by providing them with punctual deliveries of our products and services. This can be achieved by our stringent allocation planning as well as marketing and production planning with elimination of waste in every aspect.

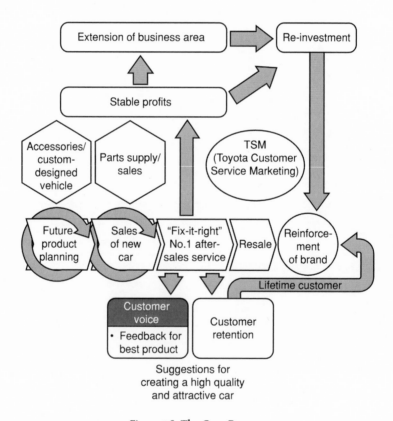

Figure 26: The Own Process

This dedication is also applicable to our final process of "Own." Customer trust and loyalty is enhanced by our providing a reliable framework of after-services, such as repairing any technical problems when and where it is most convenient for our customers. Through providing regular maintenance and our handling of their complaints with a high degree of sincerity in a timely manner, customers may say to themselves, "next time, I am going to purchase a Toyota car." Such an opportunity of reselling our products is the gateway to achieving "Customer Retention" practices, also known as "Own." Based on such considerations, our objective in the process of "Own" is focused upon "After-Services that Lead to Customer Retention."

Practices

What kind of real practices are being carried out to realize the objectives set for each of the five processes? The Silver Book clearly explains our action plan to do just that. The fifth process of "Practices" defines marketing strategies and policies that ought to be carried out while reacting to and being sensitive to any subtle marketing needs and changes. In the process "Search," the action plan defines our actions with a focus on "market communication." In the process of "Visit," it defines our actions based on our marketing structure in terms of locations of each dealership and sales person. The process of "Purchase," emphasizes "marketing activity and customer care."

In the process of "Obtain," the focus is on "supply-demand management operation." The process of "Own" describes the importance of "after-service." In every process, Toyota focuses the action plan to effectively reinsure its position as a "Power Brand" (brand that receives overwhelming support from customers) through effectively utilizing their unique enforcement of policies and marketing techniques. For your reference, I will present a visual layout of the five processes, followed by an action plan for each process, on the next four pages using landscape diagrams.

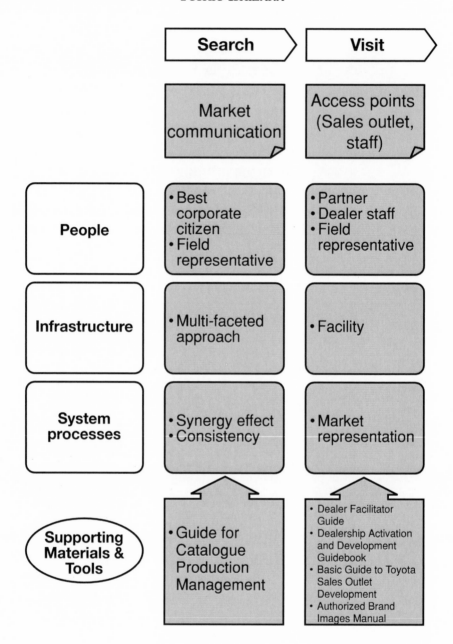

Figure 27: Visual Layout of the Five Processes

Purchase	Obtain	Own
Sales activities and administration	Supply and demand management	After-sales service
• Frontline quality • Field representative	• Field representative	• Lifetime customer • Field representative
• Customer information system	• Order management system	• Feedback for best product
• Timely information flow • Distributor support	• Sales plan • Dealer orders and production schedule • Allocation schedule • Vehicle delivery	• TSM (Toyota Customer Service Marketing)
• Lean Distribution Manual (Dealer Management) • Sales Process Control Board • Mobile tools • SFA (Sales Force Automation)	• Lean Distribution Manual (Demand & Supply, Logistics) • COSMOS (Comprehensive Overseas Sales Management & Operation System)	• TSM Operation Manual • TOPSS (Toyota Parts and Service System)

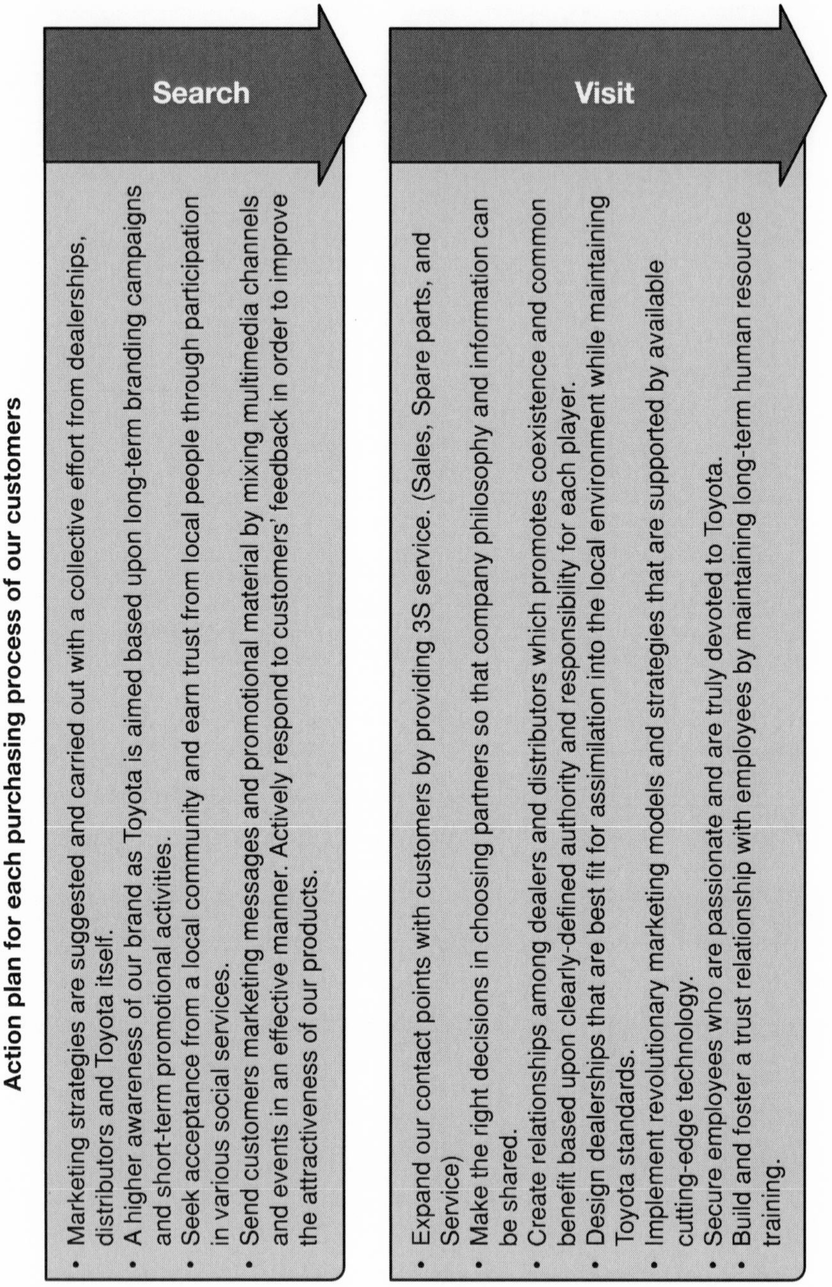

Action plan for each purchasing process of our customers

Search

- Marketing strategies are suggested and carried out with a collective effort from dealerships, distributors and Toyota itself.
- A higher awareness of our brand as Toyota is aimed based upon long-term branding campaigns and short-term promotional activities.
- Seek acceptance from a local community and earn trust from local people through participation in various social services.
- Send customers marketing messages and promotional material by mixing multimedia channels and events in an effective manner. Actively respond to customers' feedback in order to improve the attractiveness of our products.

Visit

- Expand our contact points with customers by providing 3S service. (Sales, Spare parts, and Service)
- Make the right decisions in choosing partners so that company philosophy and information can be shared.
- Create relationships among dealers and distributors which promotes coexistence and common benefit based upon clearly-defined authority and responsibility for each player.
- Design dealerships that are best fit for assimilation into the local environment while maintaining Toyota standards.
- Implement revolutionary marketing models and strategies that are supported by available cutting-edge technology.
- Secure employees who are passionate and are truly devoted to Toyota.
- Build and foster a trust relationship with employees by maintaining long-term human resource training.

Figure 28: Action Plan for the Five Processes

Purchase

- Provide a high level of expert advice and sincere attitude towards customers based on their specific needs.
- Team based selling activities among dealerships and each sales person. Provide clear delivery information and compliance at all times.
- Set appropriate goals for each staff/team members depending on their respective skill level and provide assessment for reviews.
- Processes in conducting business negotiation must be open and transparent.
- Provide practical educational curriculum and tools that reflect the feedback from the floor.

Obtain

- Create marketing methods designed to catch marketing trends or fads in a timely manner.
- Distribution of inventory stock to dealers must be carried out only for the purpose of maximizing their sales opportunity.
- Eliminate Muri (overburden), Muda (waste) and Mura (unevenness) by a collaborative effort of both sales and production departments.
- Provide and maintain transparency of standardized stock distribution among dealerships so that existing inventory can be shared fairly and in a flexible manner.
- Allocate cars in a Just-In-Time fashion.
- Manage accounts receivable in conjunction with status of deliverable cars.

Own

- In conducting repair and maintenance jobs, "fix-it-right first time" is needed to acquire life-time customers.
- Reselling opportunities can be enhanced by interlocking sales and services.
- Customer feedback is properly reported back to R&D to improve the quality and to make the best matching cars in the future.

Figure 29: Toyota's Responsibility to Dealers

The Best Results Cannot Be Achieved Only By Toyota

One thing that we must remember is that our distributors have their own responsibilities as part of the greater Toyota organization, the same way that Toyota itself has its own to fulfill at all times. The best franchise system can be established by fully acknowledging the respective responsibilities of each sector and developing specific policies and appropriate tasks and activities.

What are the main responsibilities of Toyota in this respect?

There are five areas:

Clearly define both global short-term and long-term policies and strategies.

Develop and supply products that truly reflect changing market needs.

Suggest fundamental sales operations and support implementation of such operations.

Plan and maintain human resource training that supports Information Technology upon which our sales and marketing are critically dependant.

Archive know-how and examples from distributors in each country and create opportunity to widely share such valuable information.

On the other hand, the main responsibilities of distributors are as follows:

Maintain and enhance desirable and healthy relationships with dealers.

Share objectives, challenges, and coordination of policy implementation through face-to-face communications.

Practice "3Cs for Harmony" (*Communication, Consideration* and *Cooperation*)

Provide transparency and a reward system for dealers that leads to better results.

Share authority over decisions and policies.

Support dealerships in achieving endless continuous improvement.

Carry out marketing strategies in a timely manner.

Deploy policies and planned marketing activities based only on PDCA principle. (Plan-Do-Check-Action)

Introduce synchronization between sales and production while aiming at a condition where desirable products can be sold at anytime without difficulties.

Realize a supply-demand cycle in sales with a high rate of turnover.

Create a mechanism in which the distributor is constantly supporting frontline dealerships by remembering their collective spirit as "Radar for All of Toyota."

Promote field activities based on the principle of genchi-genbutsu.

Build a foundation where dealers can pro–actively promote continuous improvement (kaizen) at the actual place of sales (genba).

Provide customers with the best possible car-life support so that you will be able to capture their hearts and earn lifetime customers by complying with "Customers Come First" policy.

Provide feedback from the shop floor of distributors.

Build effective marketing processes which reflect the needs of the actual place (genba).

Practice information sharing and continuous improvement based on the team spirit mindset.

PDCA Cycle in Sales and Marketing

I am going to explain in detail the PDCA cycle that I described in the last section. After all, the essence of Toyota's sales and marketing system is the result of their endless continuous improvement effort with an unbreakable connection with the PDCA cycle. PDCA stands for Plan — Do — Check — Action. The cycle represents a comprehensive process of innovation through continuous improvement derived from careful planning and execution of plans, as well as analyzing every outcome of such actions. To be more precise, I will illustrate each process.

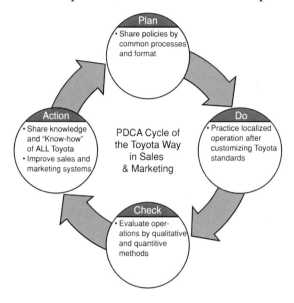

Figure 30: Toyota's PDCA Cycle

Plan

Share policies through common processes using a common format.

Do

Develop localized operations after customizing Toyota practices while maintaining the standards.

Check

Evaluate various operations in terms of both stability and sufficiency.

Action

Aim at upgrading and improving the systems of

sales and marketing by sharing the intelligence
and know-how of all of Toyota.

With these in mind, continuous improvement is being supported locally using three media:

1   Providing instruction manuals

2   Providing useful checklists

3   Organizing workshops

Through these, the sales and marketing system continues to evolve on a daily basis. In order to ensure the effective functionality of the PDCA cycle every person must establish a mechanism for making problems and their causes visible, and a common ownership, in order to achieve positive results. Through this process advancement becomes possible and valuable experiences can be shared. Every situation or issue needs to be evaluated *quantitatively* on a regular basis as much as possible. It is equally important to evaluate the level of customer satisfaction, as well as both administrative and management conditions. These are multidirectional and systematical uses of quantitative metrics and analytical tools, also known as "Key Performance Indicators." As a result, problems can be discovered at an early stage and an evaluation of solutions to such problems can take place with great accuracy.

What is the True Excellence of Toyota?

So far, I have described the essence of the Silver Book. In the process of compiling the book, a number of heated discussions had taken place to answer an important question, "How is Toyota innately different from other companies?"

Our honest answer to that question is, "Toyota not only talks about ideas, they also carry out their ideas in order to realize their objectives." What has been written in the Silver Book is nothing of special value as far as I am concerned. Every corporation understands that their customers are the most important element in their business and that effective communication with customers is the key to their future success. The question is whether a corporation has the capability of actually carrying out what they believe to be important.

As I mentioned before, Toyota sells cars in 170 different countries. Distributors are located in many countries, under which hundreds of dealers are selling our products on the frontline. With this collective mechanism of "All-Toyota (Dealer-Distributor-Toyota)" securely in place, Toyota holds a great level of pride and strength in incorporating their visions and missions into their day-to-day operations with a great level of sincerity.

If that is true, how did Toyota earn their collective mindset? Why do the philosophies described in the Silver Book continue to be implemented in 170 countries with a great level of continuity? I am going to clarify that in the following chapters.

CHAPTER 3

REINFORCING SALES AND MARKETING
ORGANIZATION BY BUILDING A PROCESS

Real Practices in Implementing the Sales & Marketing System

In order to effectively share the fundamental DNA of Toyota's sales and marketing methods, a document that defined Toyota's pioneering principles became necessary. Thus the creation of the Silver Book. Even though we knew the Silver Book would become "the bible" for sales and marketing, reading the contents alone would not be enough.

This is because the underlying philosophy of the Silver Book can only be adapted in a genuine manner on the genba, where the work is done. Only when workers, dealers, and distributors realize that our sales and marketing principles are designed for their own benefit, will they grasp the true message of the Toyota Way. To facilitate this idea into reality, we began to define the ideal condition to find the problems that stood in our way.

The first problem was that standardization of sales and marketing activities was extremely challenging, as it heavily depended on human interactions among unique individuals. I will explain how we overcame this problem later.

The second problem was that distributors and dealers across the world possess their own practical knowledge without any opportunities to share and benefit from each other. As far as the Toyota production system is concerned, the practical knowledge was collected and sorted out at the production research department. They, in turn, would make important decisions for building new factories and training employees responsible for running those factories. Standardized knowledge and techniques that have been continuously improved by Japanese factories over many years were successfully implemented in other parts of the world by the production research department.

However, practical mechanisms and techniques of the marketing system were extremely hard to collect and share as practices are localized and unique from one another depending on the region of the world. In order to solve this problem, we instituted an organization that collects our internationally-dispersed practical knowledge and standardizes Toyota's sales and marketing operations into a systematic process through specialized policies and programs. As I mentioned before, in July of 2002, we designated the Global Knowledge Center to play this very role. It is located at the University of Toyota (UOT) in California.

UOT is Toyota Motor Sales U.S.A., Inc.'s corporate university, established in 1998, and is designed to continuously develop effective methods for training American Toyota and dealer employees. The UOT is designed not only to bring together various educational programs developed by Toyota operations across the nation, but also to create more than two hundred innovative training curriculums on the topics of product knowledge, marketing processes, and leadership nurturing. UOT trains expert education advisors who have had previous work experience at Toyota to be able to train young employees. As a result, distributors not only from the US, but also all over the world have contacted the UOT for getting their questions answered and requested on-site consultations.

Figure 31: University of Toyota Instituted in 1998

©Toyota Motor Corporation
Used with permission. Permission does not imply endorsement.

While we could have integrated the GKC (Global Knowledge Center) into the UOT to serve the overall objectives, we chose not to do so. We established the GKC independently from the UOT in order to maintain its neutrality, so as not to be unduly influenced by any group and fulfill the purpose of the GKC as much as possible. At the time, the UOT was already recognized as an institute founded by the Toyota Motor Sales, U.S.A., Inc. (TMS, U.S.A.) and we wanted to prevent people from assuming that the GKC was something that the TMS, U.S.A. established for their own reasons.

Our consensus was that the GKC, having Toyota knowledge and expertise from all over the world, should always take a neutral stance. This neutral position was absolutely essential for promoting horizontal lines of communications amongst equals by eliminating biased opinions from any country and bringing down barriers between unique and diverse corporate cultures.

Overview of the Global Knowledge Center	
Purpose	• To collect examples of specific mechanisms and techniques of sales and marketing from every region of the world. • Standardize, Systematize and Share the processes of Toyota sales and marketing worldwide.
Location	• California
Foundation Date	• July 2002
Organizational structure	• Executive Committee (consisted of 4 members.) • Steering Committee (consisted of 9 members.) • Global Champions (consisted of approx. 20 members.)
Native country of members	• Japan • China • The United States • Africa • Europe • Asia • Oceania • Middle East
Workshop Curriculum	• The Toyota Way of Sales and Marketing (2-day course) • Toyota Values (1-day course) • Study of the Lexus Brand (7-day course), and so on.
Publications	• "Best Practice Bulletin" • "Global knowledge Website" • Other corporate newsletters, and so on.

Figure 32: Overview of the GKC

To maintain this neutrality, the GKC members were chosen in such a way that every region of the world was represented. Representatives were chosen not only from Japan or the Americas, but also from 6 other different regions of the world such as Europe, Oceania, China, Asia, the Middle East, and Africa, creating a unique panel of international participants. The GKC collects successful empirical data from Toyota operations scattered across the world in order to provide findings about the actual place of sales and marketing (genba) and in return, provides useful feedback and maintains practical training programs upon which Toyota employees are being trained. The GKC is the instrument for defining Toyota's realistic values and is truly a "global core," having overcome both cultural and geographical boundaries.

Purpose

To collect examples of specific mechanisms and techniques of sales and marketing from every region of the world.

Standardize, Systematize, and Share the processes of Toyota sales and marketing worldwide.

Location

California

Organizational structure

Executive Committee (consisted of 4 members.)

Steering Committee (consisted of 9 members.)

Global Champion (consisted of approx. 20 members.)

Native Countries of Members

Japan

United States

Europe

Oceania

China

Africa

Asia

Middle East

Available Workshops

The Toyota Way of Sales and Marketing (2-day course)

Toyota Values (1-day course)

Study of the Lexus Brand (7-day course)

Publications

"Best Practice Bulletin"

"Global Knowledge Website"

Other corporate newsletters

Designating Preachers for Spreading the Toyota Way in Sales and Marketing

Figure 33: First Group Photo GKC Champion Conference

Since the GKC consisted of a small group, we needed to set up additional groups of experts whose role was also to promote the Toyota Way in Sales and Marketing across the world. In other words, these experts were designated as preachers and were referred to as "Champions." They were selected primarily from distributors with a high volume of sales record, as well as from those that maintained a commanding role for each specific region.

The "Champions" were to provide critical support in developing new marketing territories. The prerequisites for becoming a Champion were that he or she proved to have had a wide range of knowledge and experiences as well as exhibited strong leadership characteristics in order to positively influence every member of the organization. These were chosen from a variety of disciplines involved in sales and marketing activities. As a result, competent supervisors from sales, marketing, and logistic departments were selected to be Champions. Approximately 20 Champions were chosen from such countries as the USA, Canada, Brazil, France, Germany, Italy, U.K., Australia, South Africa, Saudi Arabia, Taiwan, China, India, Indonesia, and Thailand.

Their charter encompasses the following roles and responsibilities:

> Spread the Toyota Way in Sales and Marketing around the world and perform a coaching role to ensure implementation.

> Function as an information window and coordinate activities and programs organized by the GKC.

> Match universal programs and training materials prepared by the GKC with unique requests and specific objectives formulated by various

distributors.

Provide distributors with useful suggestions and
advice so that understanding towards the value
and effectiveness of the GKC can be deepened.

In addition, the Champions from around the world assemble once every year for the "Champion Conference" in order
to exchange their ideas openly. The conference was primary
designed for Champions to share their knowledge, participate
in discussions and build a strong network. In its earlier stage,
upon the launch of the GKC, their conference focused on building strong relationships among the key distributors.

Figure 34: TWSM Discovery Program:
"Genchi Genbutsu" Experience

As the conferences were repeated many times, the participants became much more focused on reporting the best practices
of their dealers and distributors. They also did careful analysis

of how the Toyota Way in Sales and Marketing was being re-flected upon the actual operations. They also concentrated on actively exchanging their new innovative ideas and evaluating Toyota's future direction so that customer needs are always met and provided with the true value of Toyota's products and services.

Figure 35: A Snap Shot of TWSM
Workshop, Hosted by GKC

Utilization of Multi-media

With support of the Champions, the GKC has taken many other approaches in order to convey the realistic value of the Toyota Way in Sales and Marketing to distributors in each country. For example, as far as educational programs are concerned, a wide range of detailed classes and workshops are coordinated and are available to provide suitable training to employees so that every position has objectives associated with it. New staff and managers are given an 8-day entry level course "TWSM (The Toyota Way in Sales and Marketing) Discovery Program."

Figure 36: Best Practice Bulletin: Capturing Knowledge
for the Global Knowledge Website

This course is designed to invite newly-hired Toyota employees with a high level of potential to come to Japan and provide them with a program known as "Experience Genchi-genbutsu." This provides them with an opportunity to learn the comprehensive history of Toyota and the Toyota Way at its birthplace. Manager-level employees with a sufficient level of experience with distributors are provided with a 2-day workshop known as "TWSM Workshop." This workshop is designed to provide them with an opportunity to develop advanced training skills for introducing future applications of the Toyota Way in Sales and Marketing and for discussion.

This is an extremely valuable opportunity for trainers from around the world to be evaluated and improve upon their own training strategies and techniques. There is also a "Supply and Demand Workshop" that teaches supply-demand operations based on the Toyota Way in Sales and Marketing. The content of this workshop is extremely high level. It starts by describing how the Toyota production system conducts Lean manufacturing and successfully reduces inventories. The course then explains how these techniques tie in with the Toyota Way in Sales and Marketing and places the orders received from customers, thus directing production for the delivery of the final products.

Figure 37: Global Knowledge Website

©Toyota Motor Corporation
Used with permission. Permission does not imply endorsement.

As I explained so far, the GKC develops and makes available various programs depending on the knowledge and skill level of the trainees. The GKC also has many useful informative tools, of which the major representative is the "Best Practice Bulletin."

The bulletin gathers and redacts successful examples received from Toyota global operations and provides feedback to other branches in return. It is a monthly publication and is circulated to every distributor around the world. For example, the bulletin once wrote about a distributor in Saudi Arabia whose storage warehouse for parts was completely destroyed by fire and described in detail how the distributor immediately recovered their customer service operations as well as restoring procurement of the necessary parts. The bulletin is full of such examples, illustrating how distributors around the world have built innovative solutions to achieve continuous improvement.

It is an extremely effective knowledge–sharing tool for everyone as its descriptive and informative writing style allows them to grasp the methodology and thinking processes of their colleagues. Workers often feel a sense of togetherness with other Toyota workers in other countries and tell themselves, "I had no idea how a certain problem could be resolved by such innovative solutions" or motivate themselves by saying "Our office needs to try harder so that our story will be published in the Bulletin someday..."

The "Best Practice Bulletin" can also be accessed via internet. Our "Global Knowledge Website" contains an accumulation of Toyota know-how. It provides a direct link to the "Best Practice Bulletin" as well as newsletters, online training materials, and the most updated product information and technical knowledge.

In addition, results from academic research dealing with collective industrial knowledge, in collaboration with Stanford University and Hitotsubashi University, is being utilized as an effective tool for sharing our best practices across the world. It was our intention to make our case studies available not only internally, but also externally to other companies through the use of internet.

What if other companies steal ideas and knowledge from Toyota?

I believe that our information can only be used as reference and doubt that it can simply be copied by other companies. I believe that a successful implementation cannot be achieved unless a strong foundation of corporate culture is established in advance to appreciate the true virtue of a given system. Without it, an implementation would be only superficial even for the Toyota Production System. I strongly believe that both the Toyota production and marketing systems are built on the unique corporate culture of Toyota.

Basis of Toyota's Sales & Marketing System is a "Glocal" Perspective

What is the corporate culture of Toyota?

The answer to this question can be derived by understanding how Toyota was able to standardize human communications, which is the foundation for sales and marketing activities. The most prominent characteristic of Toyota's corporate culture is the doctrine of genchi-genbutsu, which involves solving a problem while looking at the actual item on the actual place, as well as repeating "Why" five times. As a result, the true cause of a problem can be discovered beyond the symptoms by observing the actual item, at the actual place, after simply asking yourself why repeatedly.

I was taught — and continue to teach — that this simple habit of Toyota is, in essence, the foundation of the Toyota Way. Every nation has its unique history and business culture which differ drastically from all others. Such different cultures cannot be fully comprehended by conducting research and discussions as long as you remain in your own country. The real issues and cause of a problem can be recognized only by going to the actual place and observing the actual conditions with your own eyes and talking directly with affected people in the actual place.

It reminds me of the American saying, "Never judge others

until you walk a mile in their shoes."

If you did not make this important effort, what is considered the best in Japan would be forced upon others elsewhere. This would trigger less than desirable responses and solutions would fall short of what could be achieved otherwise. Needless to say, this would make our jobs more difficult.

Loyalty is extremely important for humans to continue with their lives. No matter how large our operations become or how rapidly the globalization of our economy continues to be, being a global organization cannot be considered to be a true globalization without paying a significant level of consideration to local people and their unique culture. Many Japanese business associates have experienced a new array of issues which are often brought about by exporting what could be considered to be global knowledge and techniques and implement them in other cultures without any localization effort. If we find something domestically that has a potential to hold great applicability and could benefit other countries, we must make any necessary adjustment and improvement so that other countries can benefit from it as much as your country did.

The challenge is to be global and local at the same time. There are two basic concerns:

> Avoid any contradictions or animosity between entities by creating a mechanism that ensures harmony on a higher dimension.

> Innovate policies and actions that follow the rules of the local environment.

"Think Globally and Act Locally." This is the only way to achieve the desired results in any case.

My favorite terminology "Glocal" is often used nowadays to describe this important concept. I have always recognized this

"Glocal" attitude as one of the positive outcomes of Toyota's traditional "Genchi-genbutsu" principle for the 21st century. I have always told myself that decisions had to be made by visiting the actual place and talking to the actual people. I made it a rule to both myself and the company that every one of our principles and methodologies had to be based on this "Glocal" attitude at all times.

Figure 38: Think Global, Act Local

©Toyota Motor Corporation
Used with permission. Permission does not imply endorsement.

If we approach problems with a decision based upon our biases and assumptions, it would be impossible to ask for open-mindedness from others. Both sides must be willing to maintain open communications and share information and circumstances of the genba so that future directions and solutions that are mutually beneficial to both parties can be reached. Although this can be a time-consuming process, it is extremely important to create opportunities where everyone is equally respected and satisfied with a decision, no matter how much time and work is required.

By understanding the importance of this attitude and implementing our actions based on the sense of the "Glocal" process, the Toyota Way in Sales and Marketing can become standardized in 170 different countries in spite of differences in business cultures and marketing channels, as well as unique needs of each customer.

Having said all of the above, I cannot stress enough that effective communication betwen among distributors and dealerships from each country is extremely important. In other words, a trusting relationship among staff must be established with a great deal of devotion on the part of each individual before our knowledge and techniques can be successfully shared.

Executives Come Tumbling onto the Shop Floor

Even though some Toyota USA employees have had experience with other automobile companies, every employee agrees to the sense of solidarity and that "the strength of Toyota comes from the fact that a face-to-face communication is always maintained between Toyota headquarters in Japan and other Toyota operations across the world." Toyota USA holds a board of director's meeting twice a year with the participation of 10 or so executive directors visiting from Japan. In addition, when executives go on a business trip to foreign countries, after completing their business meetings, they go out of their way to visit as many dealers as possible so that the voice from an actual marketplace can be heard. They acknowledge that talking directly with dealers that are exposed to customers, and know their customer needs, is the best source for creating effective marketing strategies.

Such a thorough implementation of the "Genchi-genbutsu" principle creates a strong relationship of mutual trust among Toyota employees on the frontline and, as a result, is being ingrained into the core of Toyota's genba around the world. For example, when a new marketing campaign is about to take place in the US, Germany, or wherever it happens to be, it is presented to the dealerships in each country to make sure that their ideas and modifications are reflected adequately in the campaign. Such a marketing campaign is based upon the collaborative effort of every dealership and turns out to be much more effective and meaningful than ones that are forced by the headquarter's office.

In summary, the fundamental principles of the Toyota Way in Sales and Marketing are a thorough implementation of the genchi-genbutsu philosophy and Toyota's "Glocal" responsibilities. At the same time, every decision must be made by building confident teams, with mutual respect between business partners who make endless efforts towards finding the common ground.

Importance of Effective "Off-site Meetings"

How do we deal with other people?

How do we nurture employees?

Activities of sales and marketing are heavily influenced by human interaction with these questions in mind. Various opportunities need to be explored in order to deepen human communications. I have always acknowledged that such opportunities need to be arranged according to the different circumstances and requirements, such as official or private meetings or small or large scale conferences.

The Toyota "World Convention" is the biggest official event that takes place once every 4 years with participating distributors from more than 140 countries. The convention provides various forums that bring about a unified consensus upon the future. An "All-Toyota" mentality among participants and a commitment to complying with that mindset is made by each participating distributor. The convention has some other fun activities as well as exhibitions of new automobiles and receptions that provide relaxing atmospheres in which participants can mingle with one another in order to build relationships.

For small-scale opportunities, off-site meetings are a most effective method. I often participated in such meetings when I was the president of TMS, U.S.A. I remember occasions where 20-25 participants would stay at a resort for a weekend for the purpose of casually exchanging ideas on a specific agenda or critical matter.

It started with self-introductions and group discussions followed by a dinner on Friday night. Saturday was spent relaxing together while playing golf, tennis, or fishing, during which each participant grew closer and closer. We built in a mechanism to intentionally put conflicting members in the same group to provide them with an opportunity to continuously improve their relationship. As for the critical matters, five different agenda items were introduced and each group was given one specific item to discuss in detail.

The very first item involved debating about what visions and missions should be considered for TMS U.S.A. as a whole. I was extremely interested in the outcome of this debate as we agreed that goals should be finalized not by me, as the president, but by everyone. Participants were extremely enthusiastic about the debate as their opinions and ideas were taken into account in determining the corporate policy. As a result, the debate ended with many good innovative ideas and the final decision for the corporate vision was reached. The conclusion was to be the "Most Successful and Respected Car Company in the USA." Consequently, the productivity of this debate was proven by the fact that this vision was widely approved across the world and the Silver Book currently introduces it as "to become the most successful and respected car company in each country."

Another agenda was to redefine what we mean by our "customers." I was surprised to learn in that some of our office employees considered the dealerships to be also our customers. Not so! Our dealerships should be considered our business partners, and not customers. A solid scrum among dealerships, distributor, and Toyota as one entity is the most fundamental prerequisite for keeping Toyota alive. A common assumption I have heard is that dealerships are Toyota's only customers, as we provide them with finished products and consumers (eventual true customers) have nothing to do with Toyota since dealers directly deal with the final consumer. This view must be eliminated and replaced with a clearer understanding.

What is Important is to Create Opportunities for Open-Communication

At off-site meetings, I took plenty of time in explaining that dealerships are not our customers, but are our indispensable business partners by saying,

"Sales are not completed until our products are in the hands of consumers. Until then, such consumers are equally the true customers for both dealers and Toyota itself."

By openly discussing such significant topics carefully and freely, I have always felt that the participants were able to build up a positive attitude while making a commitment to comply with their own decision in a collective manner. As you already know, weekends are usually reserved for spending time with family and friends in the USA. I admit that some participants gave me a hard time for having them attend meetings on a weekend. However, I convinced them to attend meetings by promising that, even though their weekend was away from their families, it would be an exciting and rewarding experience and that they would be able to return home with a great sense of accomplishment. Using this rationale, I got my way for a while. However, after the second time around, executives were more than willing to voluntarily sacrifice their weekends for the meetings, leading me to believe that discussions from the meetings have brought them a greater sense of fulfillment and self-esteem.

Another similar example is when I go on a business trip to Japan with my American colleagues. I would ask them on Friday after work: "Please do me a favor and spend some time with me this weekend. Let's throw a party on the Island of Atami (Hatsushima) on Friday night. I want to show you the Japanese way of working hard, so to speak." Then, I would take them to a beautiful island for a short stay to enjoy some karaoke and have a relaxing time in the hot springs. Rarely have I received any backlash from them for having accepted my invitation. Instead, they received my invitation warmly. This traditional relationship among Japanese coworkers must have appeared quite refreshing to American colleagues. I understand that anyone would get fed up with routine work all the time. However, to a certain extent, if an opportunity can give workers a sense of involvement and psychological rewards, even Americans will show their willingness to spend time with coworkers, even on weekends.

In rare cases, I had to confront some of my coworkers who could not necessarily fit into this casual "off-site meeting" environment. To break the ice for them, I came up with my own strategy. I asked my wife to invite wives of both Japanese and American executives and throw a lunch party. Sometime later, the wives became close with one another through these lunch parties. We then arranged a reception inviting both the wives and their husbands. In a situation like this, my coworkers who were usually conservative and introverted were extremely relaxed and broke down inhibitions to show their willingness to cooperate. In this case, opportunities to provide workers with an effective communication environment where true feelings can be exchanged must be made available by all means possible.

Such opportunities are especially important when different cultures and circumstances of participants need to be taken into consideration. I often emphasized to the executives that the important thing to remember here was *"Inclusiveness* (a connotative relationship that welcomes as many people into the team as possible) and not *Exclusiveness* (a clannish relationship that promotes separation among people)."

Unexpected Method that Enriched Team Solidarity

For the propose of promoting a higher awareness of teamwork in the work environment, I introduced a unique Japanese sport called *Ekiden*. Ekiden is basically a marathon relay race enjoyed by many Japanese athletes, especially on New Year's day with one of the biggest competition being the "Hakone Ekiden." In Japan, Toyota also organizes the company Ekiden competition every December with about 200 relay teams participating from Toyota factories and offices from all over Japan. There are no Ekiden competitions in the US. However, many Americans enjoy jogging and I have seen many of my American coworkers going for a run on the company premise during lunch breaks and after work. Some of them told me that they were training for the Los Angels or Honolulu Marathons. This made me wonder, "What if we created an Ekiden team with American employees and fly them over to Japan to compete in an Ekiden race?" Needless to say, winning the race was not my primary concern. The true value of this idea was to organize a collaborative team with our own athletes and participate in a tradition that has been nurtured by Toyota in Japan. Consequently, 6 male and 2 female athletes were chosen and flown over to Japan combining a business trip to do some real work—such as factory tours and discussions—as well as casually participate in the Ekiden competition. The team performed better than we expected, coming in 120th out of about 200 participating teams. This surprising result started an Ekiden boom among Toyota operations all over the world, and triggered a strong desire to participate in any future Ekiden competitions. Unfortunately, not every request made from Toyota's operations could be met due to limited number of teams which can be registered. Therefore, we have set up a screening process to single out the best athletes from selected countries to fly to Japan.

This example serves to illustrate how participation in community events can bring everybody together. Such Japanese tradition or culture is well accepted among foreigners when it is properly introduced. I felt it is also important to remind ourselves of our roots in Japan, even though Toyota has become big and global. This is one of my "Global" applications.

Effective Communication is Up to Our Ingenuity

Many effective communication tools can be found if we put our heart into it. I have made it a rule to participate in departmental meetings and visit work sites whenever I had a chance. I have also made a great effort in leading training for new employees and made myself always available by holding Q & A sessions with dozens of new employees every year. Sometimes, I received questions that were rarely asked in Japan, such as "Do I get to become the president one day?," which I found quite astonishing and unique to the United States.

Close communications among offices and dealers in major cities could be managed in the same manner. However, I was worried that communication among approximately 2,000 employees in every part of the country could become much less accessible due to the spatial and geographic characteristics of the USA. To solve this problem, we have organized an annual two-week tour that we call a "Town Hall Meeting." The tour travels to major US cities and regional "Dealer Council" conferences with the participation of representatives from dealerships across the country, in order to exchange reports on business performances and provide expert guidance in setting sales goals. This setting also created opportunities to have face-to-face interactions in a Q & A format. Such interactions became quite heated and the discussions were very valuable experiences. Participants were allowed to challenge each other directly by exchanging their honest opinions and critical concerns as illustrated by the following conversation.

"This particular dealership has a reputation of providing terrible customer service. I urge you as the president to drastically improve the quality of services right away."

"You may be right in saying that it is a responsibility of the president. However, I am sure you know there are about 1,200 Toyota dealerships and 200 Lexus dealerships. It is next to impossible to manage 1,400 locations all by myself. You are a Toyota employee, are you not? It is your responsibility as well. If you realize something is wrong, you have to take the initiative on your own. You owe that to Toyota."

A passive communication method such as "Teaching" does not lead to true positive results. Opportunities for "Learning," can be achieved by exchanging perspectives with one another. Mutual understanding can yield employees' commitment towards their work and loyalty for their company. Every time I was asked to give a speech, I always made sure that there was an opportunity for having direct communication with listeners as much as time could allow. I would spend three days preparing my answers to some of the questions I knew I would get and wanted to elaborate. I did not mind the extra work at all. I acknowledge that nothing is more important than maintaining open and close communications with my fellow business partners.

Articulate Your Opinions in the Simplest Way

An effective line of communication cannot be established just by listening closely to what others have to say, but also by expressing your own opinions in a concise manner. Then, how can we convey our intention to others with positive results? The answer is "Express your opinion in a simple and straight-forwarded manner without any tricks or deception." I came to this important realization when our intranet system was implemented into our offices as a communication tool in 1996. Intranet was a rare commodity back then. It was adapted to distribute information and keep every employee updated on my daily activities as president. After a while, I found it extremely interesting that manager-class employees and regular employees often showed totally different reactions to my messages. For example, when I sent out information on a speech given at a Town Hall meeting, manager-class employees immediately sent back some useful feedback and constructive criticisms while regular employees reacted pretty slowly. However, when I talked about something that was personal and tangible such as an event where Toyota cars were donated to a cancer charity group, regular employees always provided me with an overwhelming amount of their feedback. In other words, regular employees and executive-level employees have different perspectives. As employees' responsibility and position vary, their concerns and accordingly their opinions toward certain matters vary significantly. Since the intranet was originally implemented with the objective target at establishing direct communications with regular employees who were otherwise hard to reach, we made sure that information passed on via the system was always relevant and very much mindful of their differing perspectives and responsibilities. As a result, three key points must always be kept in mind:

1   Understand and appreciate the various constituencies present in the audience

2   Bring up subject matters to which listeners feel close to their hearts

3   Express your point in an easy and simple way for listeners to understand

I learned that these three factors were extremely important in order to exchange information with a solid sense that I was talking to listeners face-to-face. This important realization also made me change the style of my speeches to improve the way listeners were approached in the simplest and the most precise way, yet in a heart-felt manner. When I visit Seattle to give a speech, I often mention the success of a Japanese baseball player, Ichiro Suzuki, who plays for the Mariners baseball team. When I visit New York, I incorporate some popular local jokes in my speech. While keeping listeners entertained and making my words relevant, I must always be sure that the very point of the speech was conveyed to listeners in a clear and accurate way at all times. Therefore, nobody should fall asleep by listening to my speeches. These were my most important goals.

Win Negotiation on an Equal Relationship

Analyzing and discussing things from the same perspective is an essential rule in promoting effective communication. At the same time, we need to make sure that our distributors and dealers clearly understand the philosophy that they *are in an equal partnership with Toyota.*

If we promote an attitude where distributors and dealerships are under the umbrella of Toyota and might as well do what they were told to do, they might develop a negative perspective, which would make it impossible to establish a true partnership.

On the other hand, if there is a solid understanding that both parties are on an equal footing in the relationship, barriers caused by differences in opinion and expectations can be overcome much more easily. Negotiations do not always go as we expect and problems come with the conduct of any business. However, if a foundation of equal relationship is already established, resolution can be found. Even in conflict, by negotiating what can be compromised, organizing and exemplifying areas of disagreement, both parties can always reach a middle ground where both are fully persuaded that the final decision is fair and to their mutual benefit. If a negotiation falls apart even with these efforts, it just means that business was not to be concluded. Eliminating any emotional conflict to be regretted in the future is a must.

For example: a son of a president from a former European distributor visited me when he was on a business trip. Normally, such a visit would be unnecessary as I was already in another position. He went out of his busy schedule and made time to visit me and told me, "You have taken care of us very well. My late father always told me that he appreciated your partnership very much. Please continue our relationship in the future."

To be honest, I was quite shocked to receive this kind of treatment, as I remember that his father and I used to have severe disagreement in many cases. For example, when we were in negotiation for the purchase of one of his dealers, we had the hardest time reaching an agreement on the selling price. At the end, I took his hand and persuaded him in a forcible manner by telling him, "We are not going anywhere even if we start these negotiations over. Let's shake hands and come to an agreement, shall we? My company (Toyota) will do anything to make this work for you. So, please compromise with this price. Our negotiation is over. Let me go buy you some drinks."

After this incident, I was always worried that he hated me for making the deal against his will. If we had failed to establish an equal relationship between us, that could have been easily the case. Aversion towards Toyota for pushing the deal through could have been carried onto his son's generation and his company could have chosen to work under any company other than Toyota. However, he was far from being hateful and expressed words of gratitude to his son who came all the way to tell me just that. Our equal relationship gave him the power to forgive my forcible action by fully acknowledging Toyota and I were his true and equal partners. We always tumble over obstacles in conducting any business transactions. Our real work is about discovering how to get over these problems easily and surely. The equal relationship we nurture and respect on a daily basis shows its biggest strength when such obstacles must be torn down for our business transactions to move forward.

Become Friends with 7 Enemies

There is an old Japanese saying that goes something like, "seven enemies are waiting for you once you step outside." It basically teaches people to be careful in what is considered to be a world full of surprises. I believe that there is some truth to that, but there is another possible interpretation. "There are many people beside yourself who have different ways of thinking about a given situation." However, I would not consider those seven strangers to be my enemies. I rather think that I should expand my scope of communication so that even those with opposing opinions can be my friends.

This is even truer as far as business partners (your friends) are concerned. Sometimes you need to work with coworkers with whom there is bad chemistry. This is when you must try your hardest to faithfully seek a mutual understanding with them by improving your own communication skills. The best way is not to be emotional and reach an immature conclusion by leaving your job unfinished when you face difficult situations. In order to maintain a long-term relationship and continue to perform meaningful work with your business partners, you must build strong trusting relationships without leaving anything aside. This will give you a clear direction into the future.

I had a unique opportunity in the past to meet a not-so-popular and notorious executive manager in a European country. I was a bit apprehensive when I learned from an expatriate executive how difficult this manger could be.

"Mr. Ishizaka, the person you will meet today, everyone dislikes meeting with him. In other words, not only other company executives, but also his own subordinates who work directly under him intentionally avoid him. Are you ready to meet him?" He was indeed a bitter individual as everyone knew him to be. As I sat there, listening to what he had to say, he would utter one complaint after another about Toyota. I spent all day in his office paying close attention to what he had to say while taking down some detailed notes. As I reviewed his comments from my notes, I learned that his comments could be categorized into 20 groups or so, a mixture of complaints and demands. I read down my list to him by saying, "Did I understand your concerns correctly? Please give me some time to fix the problems."

The executive manager replied with disappointment, "Toyota people always tell me the same thing and ask me to give them some time. I have never received any resolutions and my problems keep on piling up."

Having heard this and felt his frustration, I started to see vaguely the reasons why he had been so fed up with Toyota.

Listen to All Wishes, Including Impossible Ones

My assumptions were that the executive manager was fed up with Toyota and felt that his requests were always ignored and never taken seriously. In this case, the most important thing was to persuade him that he had always been treated sincerely with attention to details and that he has been always taken seriously by me as well. I suggested to him the following, "Out of what you told me, I can answer seven items myself. The remaining items cannot be solved by my authority only. May I ask you to come to our headquarters in Japan? With your cooperation and our joint explanation on these business matters to other departments, I am confident that most of your requests will be met."

He accepted my invitation. I decided to remove his negative feeling toward Toyota by taking care of him. I took him to every department at the headquarter office throughout the day and solved his problems one by one, except for five items that were categorized as completely unreasonable demands. As for those five items, I made sure that he understood why they were impossible by providing him with solid explanations. Another expatriate executive was surprised and asked me, "How did you pull that off? You must be a patient individual. All of us are aware that his requests are always in shambles. I never understood his perspectives. How did you make him so happy?"

I gave this advice to the expatriate, "You need to change your attitude. I agree that some of the items were obviously out of the question due to his misunderstanding. If you just told him then that he was wrong, nothing could be done. You must put yourself in his shoes and listen closely to what he has to say. If Toyota can fix it, fix it immediately. If it is impossible, make sure he completely understands why by giving a thorough explanation. If you follow my rule diligently, he is most likely to show understanding."

Since the incident, I have developed a strong partnership with the executive manager. As soon as he went back to his country, I received a fax from him stating how grateful he was for our visit in Japan. The next time we had an opportunity to meet, he put his arm around my shoulder and told me, "Please come to my house for a meal, I would love for my wife to finally meet you." After all of this, he began to accept Toyota's demanding requests most of the time. After all, human beings act upon their emotions. This is true for any business person no matter which country he/she comes from. If each other's perspectives are shared with understanding, many challenges can be overcome by working together. In other words, it is true to state that most our work consists of establishing strong relationships with business partners honestly and in a step-by-step fashion. As I described before, one of the two pillar concepts of *The Toyota Way 2001* is "Respect for People." Please remember here that *Respect* and *Teamwork* are the keywords in "Respect for People" and that the Silver Book defines the "3Cs for Harmony," (*Communication, Consideration* and *Cooperation*) that is the foundation for the Toyota Way in Sales and Marketing. I hope that you understand that Toyota has repeatedly made a strong effort to implement the following principle and philosophy on a daily basis. Principle: build mutual respect among business partners and solidify promises. Philosophy: make actions based on maintaining cooperation, developing mutual understanding and respecting each other's point of view.

This is what the Toyota Way in Sales and Marketing is all about in a nutshell: a trusted business relationship.

This process is not unlike the famous quote of Abraham Lincoln: "Am I not destroying my enemies when I make friends of them?" The key is to closely listen to the other person's concerns, understand their point of view and address their concerns.

CHAPTER 4

WHY LEXUS BECAME SUCCESSFUL

Lexus is the Result of Pursuing the Toyota Way

Toyota alone sold about 8,430,000 cars worldwide in 2007. The sales almost doubled from 1997 when Toyota sold about 4,840,000 cars. This drastic increase in Toyota's sales volume has been sustained by sales that are taking place overseas. As illustrated by the figure on the next page, the domestic and international sales were about the same in 1991. However, international sales have been increasing exponentially in last 15 years, and more than 80 percent of Toyota cars are currently sold in countries outside Japan.

Toyota's largest market is the US, which accounts for more than 30 percent of the total sales. After the year 2001, the volume of sales in the US exceeded that in Japan. It is true to say that the successful US market led to a much larger success on a global scene with the sale volumes in Asia and Europe also increasing drastically.

International and Domestic Sales of Toyota

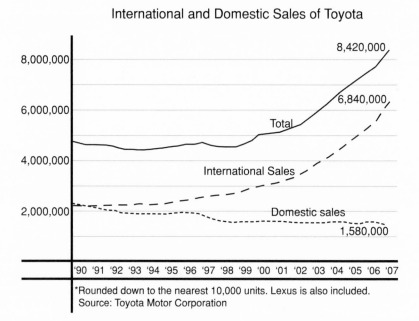

Figure 39: Domestic and International sales

Toyota's success in the US can be attributed mainly to the tremendous achievement of Lexus cars. The Lexus introduced Toyota into the luxury-car industry and helped Toyota gain a certain degree of recognition in a field where Toyota had not previously been involved. In 1989, The Lexus brand was launched into the market, targeting wealthy customers. It earned the #1 position in the US luxury-car industry in terms of the total volume sold in 2000. Since then, Lexus has continued to maintain its #1 position over eight consecutive years. The Lexus brand continues to be a popular global brand, having entered in the European market in 1993; a full-fledged marketing campaign began in 2005, in both Japan and China.

The book *The Lexus and the Olive Tree,* written by a New York Times journalist, Thomas Friedman, talks extensively about Lexus as a prominent representation for each nation's commitment toward creating an innovative and comprehensive economic system in our post-cold war environment.

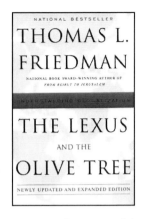

Figure 40: *The Lexus and the Olive Tree*

Personally, I feel extremely proud of the Lexus brand, not only for being a symbol of Toyota, but also for our advancement into globalization. Needless to say, the Lexus did not come about by itself. Toyota was compelled to make decisions and accept changes that went against their common sense. It was created by both the production department, which made a tremendous effort to collaborate with Toyota's technologies, and the sales department, which created meticulous marketing strategies over the years. From this point of view, I am confident to say that Lexus represents an ultimate pursuance of both the Toyota Way and the Toyota Way in Sales and Marketing.

Discontinuity in Continuity

Toyota went from producing adaptive, energy efficient, and affordable mass-market cars, to creating sophisticated, high quality cars with perfect customer service to match. I am always extremely impressed with the dedication of Mr. Eiji Toyoda (the chairman of Toyota Motor Corporation at the time) who led the whole company into breaking out of the paradigm. I can never forget my experiences in the boardroom of Toyota Motor Corporation headquarters where a number of top executives met for secret discussions. When the final decision had to be made at the end of our heated arguments, all participants held their breath to hear the words from Mr. Eiji Toyoda. The room was completely silent. His voice echoed around the room when he said, "We will follow the plan set forth by Toyota USA."

I was the Senior Vice President of Toyota Motor Sales, U.S.A., Inc. at the time. It was the very moment when our polished project for Toyota's new brand creation "Lexus" was finally approved, having overcome various objections from Toyota's headquarters in Japan. It was Toyota's monumental decision in taking this extraordinary challenge on which their future heavily depended on.

Figure 41: The Prius Hybrid

©Toyota Motor Corporation
Used with permission. Permission does not
imply endorsement.

However, it was a necessary challenge for Toyota after all. There is no leap forward if you stay on the continuum of the same old things. In order to compete on a higher level, new challenges and attempts beyond conservative practices within your comfort zone are absolutely necessary. The greatest opportunity can be gained when you strive for discontinuity from continuous routines. I strongly believe that great achievements can be gained when discontinuous ideas intentionally challenge the realm of continuity. This is true for both human beings and corporations. The creation of the Lexus brand and the hybrid car "Prius" are excellent examples of Toyota's discontinuity in its continuous reality.

Bold Decision of the Chairman, Eiji Toyoda

As I look back to the past, it was the year 1957 when Toyota entered the US market with the introduction of the "Crown" model. After that, Toyota began exporting the "Cressida (a.k.a. Mark II in Japan) and two other types of consumer-grade vehicles, the "Corolla" sedan and "Hilux" pickup truck in the 1980's. They expanded their US market share by promising high-quality products and providing comprehensive customer support. It was a time characterized by escalating gasoline prices, the oil shocks of the 1970's, and economic inflation. "Auto Trade Friction" worsened between Japan and the US due to the increasing market share of our built-up imported vehicles.

We established a 50/50 joint venture with General Motors known as NUMMI (New United Motor Manufacturing, Inc.) to fulfill the need for promoting a localized production system and meet our self-imposed measures to have automobiles assembled in the USA. Later, Toyota constructed its own assembly factory known as the TMMK "Toyota Motor Manufacturing,

Figure. 42: NUMMI Tape Cutting

©Toyota Motor Corporation
Used with permission. Permission does not
imply endorsement.

Kentucky" which was the first to be built in the US. As a result, Toyota continued to build a solid foundation in the US market and the efforts were rewarded by being evaluated as the #1 consumer brand in terms of "customer satisfaction in initial product quality" by J. D. Power and Associates, a US firm conducting market research across the nation.

However, in order to grow a larger market share in the US, Toyota believed in internal expansion. We concluded that Toyota ought to be more aggressive in the US luxury car market where profitability promised to be much larger due to higher prices given to their cars. This aspiration was considered to be a milestone and the perfect way for the expected celebration of Toyota's 50th Anniversary in 1987. Subsequently, a project named the "F1 Project" was initiated to develop Toyota's future flagship cars and proceeded its development efforts in Japan. The F1 project, which eventually became the "Lexus LS 400" project, brought all of the Toyota's improved technology together and consumed two to three times more labor and time than Toyota usually required for the development of a new vehicle.

The luxury flagship car, LS 400 was capable of a maximum speed of 250km/hr (155mph) and had a fuel efficiency of 23.5 miles per gallon (approx. 9.93km per liter). Some of its impressive features included an elegant-look, light body structure that is quiet, yet stable, and its interior design was functionally intuitive and provided a high-class feel. In order to make these features come true, six years and an investment of one billion US dollars were spent with the help of about 3,700 engineers who built 450 prototypes covering 1,000,000 miles of test driving.

When the production of the LS 400 was about to be completed, there turned out to be a bit of misunderstanding between the Japan and US offices. The Japan office assumed that the flagship car would be sold via existing sales channels. On the other hand, the US office insisted on selling the flagship car in a completely new network of dealerships supported by innovative business models, and to develop a premium brand for upper-class consumers. In 1988, an executive board meeting took place with the intent to resolve this very disagreement. The ultimate decision was with Mr. Eiji Toyoda who fully supported the position of the US office, as I mentioned before.

Bill Gates as the Targeted Customer

Why was the US office so particular about launching a new

brand? This was because they longed to differentiate Lexus from other ordinary cars. As I described in the previous chapter, Americans already had a certain impression of Toyota cars. I am not implying that their impressions were bad, however, Toyota had a strong desire to spread a message that the flagship car was not an extension of their traditional cars but that the LS 400 was a product that signified something out of the ordinary. Toyota's persistence was also a result of their elaborate marketing efforts. A specialized unit named "Lexus Team" was formed under the leadership of Mr. Yukiyasu Togo, the president of Toyota Motor Sales, U.S.A., Inc. at the time, to conduct comprehensive analysis on the most effective sales and marketing strategies to target the luxury car market. Having heard the voices of customers and suggestions received from various dealerships, every bit of information about the lifestyles and mindsets of upper-class consumers toward owning luxury cars were thought through in detail.

In order to truly understand the peculiarities of the consumer segment being targeted, about 20 Japanese engineers were sent to the US from Toyota's headquarter office. The engineers, who were well versed on the importance of the "Genchi-genbutsu" principle, experienced the "tuxedo lifestyle" of the wealthy for a long period of time. The marketing team visited houses of those who owned luxury cars and carried out people-watching at luxury hotels and high-class shopping centers. Many designed sketches for the flagship car were drawn and vetted with the public repeatedly in order to select a perfect design to suit the environment of the focus groups. Both the engineering and marketing teams concluded that the new car needed to meet the following five main requirements in terms of customers' expectations of luxury vehicles:

1   Sense of status and prestige of ownership

2   High level of quality

3 High resale values in the used car market (this is an exceptionally important factor)

4 Advanced level of performance

5 Guaranteed safety

Among these prerequisites, we were confident about items 2, 4, and 5 as they are primarily concerned with the physical attributes of our products. However, items 1 and 3 required most of our ingenuity and a unique twist. In particular, item 1 had everything to do with customer's impression of Toyota. Based upon the market research findings, we revisited our fundamental approach and tactics for the marketing of the luxury vehicle.

Our typical targeted customers for the flagship car were identified to be 47 year-old male professionals, in a specialized field, who made an average of 100,000 US dollars annually. More precisely, our targets were not those who inherited their wealth through family connections, but were those who earned a high socio-economic status by creating a wealth on their own. We chose Bill Gates, the founder of Microsoft, as representative of this newly-formed category of wealthy individuals. In contrast, BMW has been image-driven as "cars for intelligent individuals." However, our prospective upper-class customers were those who were not so attracted to owning a BMW car. Instead, they were widely influenced by the degree of practicality and true value of a given car.

Our customers often thought that it was smarter to purchase something that was better quality than a Cadillac, yet more affordable than a Mercedes. Our ultimate goal was to make customers feel that it would make perfect sense to spend an extra $10,000 dollars on top of the price of a Cadillac and save the extra $20,000-30,000 required to upgrade to a Mercedes. Therefore, prerequisite #1, providing a "sense of status and prestige of ownership" was the key for the success of the F1 Project and had to be met without exception. In order to meet this challenge, it meant establishing a new array of marketing channels that were clearly differentiated from those of ordinary Toyota.

Tremendous Success that Returned the Initial Investment within 5 Years

The very moment I heard Mr. Toyoda's decision about going in a completely new direction, I remember feeling a great deal of hope and an undeniable uncertainty in me. It felt as though Toyota was going on a voyage in a boundless expanse of ocean without a hydrographic map, so to speak. First, I thought we had to have a map of some sort. As a matter of fact, we had none and something had to be created right away. We made sure that our map considered as many approaches as possible. Many critical factors had to be considered such as analyzing who our audiences were, setting sales targets, and selling prices and determining an appropriate policy for distribution. The number of dealerships and the terms of the agreement had to be a part of any effective marketing strategies.

As for securing potential customers, we set our selling prices to provide better value than those of Mercedes so that Lexus remained more attractive. For example, the price of the first Lexus LS 400 series was deliberately set lower than that of Mercedes 300E even though it had the same or better specifications and performance than those of Mercedes 420SEL (one rank above the 300E). In order to avoid the market's typical assumption that less expensive cars meant lower quality, we provided an extended service warranty to express a high level of confidence in our products. The warranty we offered provided coverage for five years after purchasing. At the time, this was way ahead of those promoted by other competitors in the luxury car business.

The initial sales goal required to sustain this new marketing venture, was set at 20,000 cars. To put this number into perspective, the market size for upper luxury cars at that time was between 40,000 and 50,000 cars a year. This meant that it was extremely challenging for Lexus to meet the initial sales goal despite how advanced and affordable the LS 400 proved to be. Consequently, a request for the development of an additional model was put forth to reinforce the launching of the Lexus brand and increase the volume of sales under the brand. As a result, the ES 250 was introduced as the second model in the Lexus line–up after having modified the Vista series that was originally targeted for the Japanese market. Two years later, Lexus introduced into the mix the SC 300 and SC 400 that were designed in tandem with the Japanese market Toyota Soarer. Lexus sells seven different models at present time. However, the most influential models over the luxury car market were the first two models released on the launching of the Lexus brand.

Figure. 43: Lexus Line Off

©Toyota Motor Corporation
Used with permission. Permission does not imply endorsement.

The overall quality of the LS 400 was overwhelmingly appraised by the market and Lexus continued to build a positive reputation. The year following the LS 400 release, a consumer survey administrated by J. D. Power and Associates, named the Lexus to be #1 in the category of preliminary quality control. The ES 250 that struggled in the beginning was replaced by the ES 300 and became Lexus' best selling sedan. The LS 400 and

ES 250 sold more than 16,000 cars over a four month period, beginning in September of 1989 and sold as many as 64,000 cars in the following year.

In spite of the fact that our sales did not meet our initial goal, we felt strongly that we had made a solid entry into the luxury car market and expanding demand kept us moving towards our predictions. The total financial investment for putting the Lexus brand on track was approximately one billion US dollars and was surprisingly recovered within five years. Lexus dealerships across the country were also able to recover their initial investments more smoothly. Some dealerships were able to climb into the black within two years by earning a profit of about three million dollars every year. With our tremendous effort and comprehensive preparation, Lexus brand gained a strong position in the US luxury car segment. I believe that our effective planning and diligent efforts established close communication networks and infrastructures among the Lexus dealership and that this in turn helped Toyota achieve its tremendous success.

The Lexus Brand and Network of Dealership

It was not easy to create a new dealership network. Concerns from the Japanese headquarters about this matter were so substantial that they originally expressed a resistance to the Lexus brand idea put forth by Toyota Motor Sales, U.S.A., Inc. Everything depended on whether Lexus could provide customers a sense of status in owning Lexus cars, as well as offering the best-in-the-world customer support and services. In order to make this happen, we came up with an innovative mechanism for dealerships so that the level of profit was always warranted. Unless such a promise was made, dealers, especially the high-caliber ones, would be unwilling to participate in the risky challenge of selling cars under a completely different brand or might lean toward starting a discount war. There is no way can a sense of status can be generated among customers under these scenarios.

In addition, dealerships in the US could generally expect profits derived 40% from sales of new cars, 30% from repairs and maintenance, and 30% from sales of used cars. Because the Lexus brand was completely new, Lexus dealerships had no used cars and they could not rely on repair and maintenance services. Therefore they needed to be given significantly higher margins over what they would normally receive in the industry. Also, dealerships were limited in number and were placed in a way that their marketing territories did not overlap. We created a dealership-location map based on the annual incomes of every region in the territory allowing for placements in ideal locations. Furthermore, we established a close support network composed of small groups of elite salesmen.

As for the number of dealerships, we projected to have about one hundred dealerships at the launch of the Lexus brand and ultimately increase up to 200 dealerships. In selecting dealerships, we searched for those that had proven records in either selling Toyota cars or other luxury cars with a high level of customer satisfaction and exhibited an ability to adapt to the unprecedented way of launching the new brand in a flexible manner. They were selected carefully after undergoing a series of comprehensive evaluations on the basis of market share, profitability, the level of customer satisfaction received, capital strength, and business appearance.

Judging from the fact that about 1,600 applications were submitted for 200 available Lexus dealerships across the US, it is true to say that the entire car retail industry saw a great deal of potential in a new luxury brand that was introduced as "giving customers the same quality as Mercedes for the price of a Cadillac." After careful application reviews and interviews, 80 dealerships were selected as initial partners for launching Lexus. As a matter of fact, 70% of the selected dealerships were Toyota dealerships. As I had anticipated, they were much more willing to accept this extraordinary challenge based upon the strong relationships they had developed with Toyota over a number of years.

It was a tremendous challenge for each selected dealership as well. This was because we enforced the requirements that the Lexus dealers had to adopt a unified interior and exterior appearance and be equipped with designated information technology systems. The initial capital investment was between three and five million dollars. As for setting up the actual operation in each physical location, managers from the Lexus department visited every dealership to make sure that the standardized designs for interior and exterior of dealerships and installation of the required equipment had been met. In addition, we made it a rule to provide Lexus parts, including those shared with Toyota, in their own Lexus-brand packaging. This was because customers could easily see the maintenance & repair service area from the showroom. Last, but not least, we strictly followed our customer service policy to treat customers with a personal touch so that they always felt at home. Customers were provided with intimate knowledge of our products as well as that of our competitors.

Achieving Collective Goals with Supply Chain Integration

Our efforts to maintain close communications with dealerships brought positive results for our Lexus project as well. We established satellite offices at four locations in the US and assigned "field managers" who were in charge of taking care of five to 10 dealerships. In September of 1989, around the time of the release of the first Lexus models, we made sure that every dealership in their territory was visited on a daily basis.

Executive managers from the Lexus department at Toyota Motor Sales, U.S.A., Inc. also visited dealerships to observe the actual practices and receive feedback on the quality and scope of our services. By regularly talking to not only dealership managers, but other employees in charge of sales, services, accounting, and even car cleaning services, we were able to analyze conditions, identify problems, and develop continuous improvement ideas and solutions based upon the raw input from the field.

We also provided many opportunities for maintaining as much intimate communications as possible. The "National Lexus Dealership Meeting" is held once a year with the participation of 1,000 people from 200 dealerships in the US. The chairman, president, other directors, and executive managers from Toyota headquarters in Japan also attend the meeting to enhance communication and support for the yearly objectives to be achieved and the strategies to be implemented by Toyota Motor Sales, U.S.A., Inc.

As well, the "Fireside Chat Meeting" is held every year between January and February in which Lexus dealerships can present their demands and have their questions answered. Just like having an intimate conversation in front of the fireplace, the purpose of this meeting is to have open and casual discussions at all times. Top executives from the Lexus department at Toyota Motor Sales, U.S.A., Inc. and operation managers visit 12 locations in the US in order to talk face-to-face with dealers. In addition, the president of Toyota Motor Sales, U.S.A., Inc. and top executives from the Lexus department meet with regional representatives of the "National Dealership Advisory Council." It is held every year in spring and fall and each meeting lasts for three days. The purpose of the meeting is to review recommendations from each region. Such recommendations are later published along with answers from Toyota Motor Sales, U.S.A., Inc. and distributed to every dealership.

Opportunities for training have been developed and scheduled frequently along side these avenues for communication. As described in the second chapter concerning the GKC (Global Knowledge Center), The University of Toyota provides 200 training programs on various topics. We also developed a self-training program called "Lexus Lab" that can be used on a computer. Every staff member at the dealership is required to go through training every year to update their product knowledge. Expenses related to the training are shared equally by the Lexus department and dealerships. When a new model is released, dealerships are leased a brand new car to be test driven by the sales staff so that they can fully understand the advantages and true value of the car. This allows sales associates to become capable of effectively presenting the features and benefits of the car, making the appeal to customers even more persuasive.

Inventory Management System Protects the Lexus Brand

In order to communicate a unified image of Lexus brand, the content of our advertisements for both different geographical regions and market territories are kept consistent. Usually, advertisements vary depending on a goal and budget, making it becomes extremely difficult to convey a message with any consistency. We organized the "Lexus Dealer Advertising Association " (LDAA), which consists of dealership representatives who put together across-the-board advertisement to be distributed locally and nationally. As a result, our PR activities incorporated various media including national TV commercials, local newspaper advertisements, radio commercials, and many others with a great level of consistency.

As for our policies to answer changing supply and demand, we keep monitoring the stock at the dealerships slightly less than the market demand, maintaining a low volume of inventory level in their hands. In the US, there is a strong expectation among consumers that dealerships are full of stock and believe they can drive home in a brand new car on the day of purchasing it. This has led to many problems in the past among dealerships that chose to maintain a large stock and, as a result, faced problems of weak cash-flow due to their high initial investment in inventory. Such dealerships often took on short-term marketing measures such as offering unjustifiable, to-good-to-be true discount rates to sell off their inventories so that their funds could flow better and be utilized to their full potential.

We believed it was extremely important to prevent our dealerships from going down this route, so we have developed a comprehensive information system to monitor inventories at every dealership. Our regional representative office, the Lexus USA head office, and each dealership can accurately check not only the inventories but also grasp the daily sales data, as well as service contracts and other key management statistics.

It also provided us with a foundation for calculating the appropriate level of inventory as well as distribution rationale for new models among our dealerships. In the early stage of the Lexus launch we concluded that an appropriate level of inventory was 19 days. In other words, our goal was to make sure that all of the new shipments delivered to a dealership had to be sold out in 19 days, which evidently was only a third of our competitor's inventory level. In reality, Lexus attracted so many people and were so popular from the beginning that all of the stocked cars were often sold out within a week. Our "Just-In-Time" (only necessary items at necessary time in a necessary quantity) philosophy became quite useful for Lexus marketing strategy in a most unlikely way.

After-sales Services Practiced by Lexus

Lexus developed a satellite information system in addition to the computer-based information network system that I described in the last chapter. The Lexus dual communication system is linked to the headquarters in Japan, Toyota Motor Sales U.S.A., Inc. Lexus department, regional representative offices, and every single dealership located in the US for the purpose of providing and perfecting the finest after-sales service to customers. The system enabled every dealership to share the techniques of our "fix it right the first time" service, which aimed at fixing any problems that customers might have without any delay or having customers wait at all.

Lexus cars are not like ordinary cars and are an agglomeration of complex electronic components. Because of that, it is extremely difficult to perform diagnostic work if a problem occurs. At an earlier stage of operation, a number of specialized engineers were sent from Japan to each regional representative office. If a problem was detected anywhere in the US, they would be required to visit the local dealership to provide technical support and prevention of technical troubles.

However, the satellite information system allowed both dealerships and the Japanese global service center to remotely communicate and provide a "fix it right the first time" to wherever needed. For example, after detecting a problem overseas, the responsible dealership sent video footage of the defect to the global service center. Expert engineers at the global service center analyzed the problem and presented their solution on a remotely-accessed computer screen. Simultaneously, the global service center continued providing follow-up assistance in order to confirm that the problem had been solved completely. In addition, the problems and solutions that were discovered in this case would be carefully documented and broadcast to every dealership via the satellite system. New diagnostic techniques and repair guidelines developed on location (genba) are archived by the responsible regional representative office and are later consolidated into the company technical bulletin, which is also distributed to every dealer on a CD-ROM. As described so far, the dual-communication network allowed us to accumulate and share customer information in an effective manner. We required our dealerships to collect and manage information for every single customer such as their vehicle(s) information, the name of customer, where the car was purchased and what kind of after-sales services were being provided. By using this information, dealerships created a database for every sold car, sharing any information related to repairs and maintenances with other dealerships.

By understanding every detail about each customer, we were able to provide them with our finely-tuned response as well as supplying dealerships with essential components in the most efficient way. We were able to make projections for which parts were needed and when they were able to be delivered by, which allowed us to service our customers without any delay while still maintaining a low volume of inventory for parts at all times. In case a certain component needed to be delivered urgently, we allowed dealerships to bypass Toyota Motor Sales, U.S.A., Inc. and communicate directly with Japan to arrange immediate air freight to the nearest airport. Such a flexible handling of emergencies can be achieved due to the direct dual-communication system and made available between the Japanese headquarters and every single dealership. Most surprisingly, the volume of inventory for parts for Lexus dealerships was only less than a quarter of that of conventional Toyota dealerships. By this fact, you can begin to recognize the benefits of the greatest efficiency achieved that has been built into our parts distribution system and inventory management.

How Did Lexus Earn the Highest Level of Customer Satisfaction?

Lexus's high quality of services, referred to as "fix it right the first time," and the management system for supplying the necessary part based on the "Just-In-Time" principle were implemented not only to achieve the highest level of customer service, but also to meet our promise to dealerships that they would achieve a high rate of return at all times.

Ironically, Lexus cars rarely had any problems. Therefore, the dealerships could expect to earn much less profit from repair and maintenance service. Customers can bring their cars into any dealership to receive complimentary services under the provided warranty. Expenses of those services are reimbursed by Toyota to dealerships. As indicated before, 30% of the profit made by a dealership depends on providing such services. Therefore, it was extremely critical for dealerships to be convinced that their customers would say, "Lexus dealers always fix my car instantly without shortages of any parts or services, and the best part is that it's all free. I'm going to make it a rule to visit a Lexus dealership rather than any private auto mechanics from now on."

Our dealerships had to do anything they could to prevent customers from going to competitors, especially with services related to regular maintenance and repairs.

In order to enhance the level of customer satisfaction to the finest level, we provided our customers with many unique and unprecedented services in the industry. For example, we offered not only a free loaner car during a repair and towing services in an accident, but also many other services such as a complimentary car wash, gasoline fill-up and shuttle services. Lexus also paid up to $200 per night for hotel accommodations when a break-down occurred in a remote area and provided 24-hour roadside assistance. Floors in the maintenance area of a Lexus dealership were always polished and shiny which customers were able to observe through large glass windows while our mechanics enthusiastically performed inspections and maintenance. Some dealerships offered customers meal vouchers so that customers could relax while waiting for maintenance work to finish. Customer service representatives at dealerships were expected to always exercise their own initiative and creativity in seeking new services on their own, and impressed customers as a result. Lexus strongly believes that after sales services lead to an opportunity for future sales.

A survey showed that customers satisfied with their experience at a certain dealership were eight times more likely to return to the same dealership for another purchase than those who were not. J. D. Power and Associates conducted a customer satisfaction survey limited to three years of post-sales customer experiences and chose Lexus to be the #1 company nine times in 10 years starting in 1991.

"We Have Never Seen Operations with Such a High Level of Efficiency."

Let me explain to you the "Lexus Covenant" in this section. The spirit behind it entails providing services based on creating the "most advanced vehicle," building "excellent sales and marketing channels," and treating each customer as we would a guest in our home. The covenant is signed by every single manager and employee in the Lexus USA organizations as well as dealerships.

Dealerships came to realize the true meaning of the Lexus covenant when Lexus faced the first instance of a vehicle recall. The first flagship model, LS 400 suffered from three defects consecutively upon its release into the market. The defects were: misalignment of brake lights stemming from deformation of the tail light enclosure due to heat; failing disengagement of the cruise control system; and dead batteries. In a sense, these defects were quite common among newly manufactured cars. Since no injuries or accidents were caused by it the consensus at the time was to avoid recalls by all means. However, Toyota Motor Sales, U.S.A., Inc. made a point to recall these defects and announced it to the public after only three months after the introduction of LS 400. It was everyone's wish to avoid the recall, as the LS 400 was introduced with a catch phrase of being the "most reliable car created by 1,400 perfectionists," promising a luxury car of the finest quality offered at a reasonable price. The last thing Lexus wished to do was to destroy its brand image. Many other departments and dealerships showed their strong objection to our decision by saying to us, "You are intentionally destroying the image of our flagship car!" We managed to overcome their objection by replying to them, "It would be too late if any causalities were caused because of the defects."

We acted promptly to initiate the recall administration and

explained to all of our dealerships exactly how we would go about accomplishing this challenge. The existing customers who had already purchased 8,000 cars were contacted by dealerships and were informed about the situation. Toyota Motor Sales, U.S.A., Inc. also sent a sincere apology letter to every single one of the 8,000 customers. Engineers from Japan along with employees from the Toyota USA Lexus department, a total of 150 staff, formed support teams visiting dealerships in order to provide specific repair instructions as well as securing replacement components. Because the LS 400 was unprecedented and designed from scratch, most of the components were specially engineered for Lexus and were hardly shared with other existing models. We asked our suppliers to prioritize production of the essential components right away.

Under such arrangements, our recall teams visited customer's houses and picked up their cars. Customers were offered a replacement car for the duration of repair and received their car after it had been completely detailed, cleaned, and filled with gas. In some cases, the support staff flew all the way to Alaska to serve customers on location.

It took Lexus a few months to complete the recalls. Judging from the fact that Toyota had to spend a whole year to complete the same type of recalls five years before, it is true to state that Lexus performed extremely well and in a timely fashion. Ironically, our handling of the recalls led customers to have a much higher level of trust and appreciation towards Lexus. We did not receive any complaints or criticism. Instead, customers showed their trust in Lexus by saying,

> "Lexus is such a sincere company. They disclosed even the smallest problem and recalled it in such a respectful and swift manner. The main priority of Lexus is to protect our safety. Lexus would never sacrifice our interest to protect their own name."

Our dealerships were also satisfied with our decision and actions. A dealership manager once told me,

> "Toyota Motor Sales, U.S.A., Inc. delivered the necessary components on the day the recall was announced. On that very day, Lexus engineers visited our facility to train us on the repair. I have been in this industry for more than 15 years, and I have never seen an operation with such a high level of efficiency."

I strongly believe that this whole recall incident turned out to be an extremely meaningful experience for Lexus itself as it created even stronger bonds of solidarity among both dealerships and corporate departments. It revealed the true meaning of the Lexus covenant by providing an important learning opportunity to all of us. In August 1987, every staff member in the Lexus department made a collective commitment to provide highest quality of products and customer service.

Figure. 44 Lexus Covenant

The Lexus Covenant

Lexus will enter the most competitive, prestigious automobile race in the world. Over 50 years, Toyota's automobile experience has culminated in the creation of Lexus cars. They will be the finest car ever built.

- Lexus will win the race because Lexus will do it right from the start.

- Lexus will have the finest dealer network in the industry.

- Lexus will treat each customer as we would a guest in our homes.

- If you think you can't, you won't.

- If you think you can, you will!

- We can, we will.

What it Means to be Lexus

- Lexus is about polished technology and high quality production mechanisms.

- Lexus is about elegant design and performance.

- Lexus is about keeping promises to customers.

- Lexus is about taking care of customers as important individuals.

- Lexus is about providing a comprehensive and positive customer experience with professional mentality and sincerity.

- Lexus is about doing everything right from the beginning.

- Lexus is about supporting each customer on a personal level.

- Lexus is about going beyond customer expectations.

Sales Do Not Always Follow a Manual

Since the recalls, I learned that more and more dealerships have made it a practice to chorus the Lexus Covenant at the beginning of each business day. As dealerships understood the true implications of the Lexus Covenant and the philosophies behind the Toyota Way in Sales and Marketing, each dealership began to proactively provide unique customer services based upon their own initiative.

Let me give an example. A young couple that recently had purchased a Lexus was driving their new car to a hospital to give birth to their new child. However, the wife started going into labor before she reached the hospital. They ran into a nearby Lexus dealership for assistance. Staff at the dealership immediately called for an ambulance, only to find out that the wife already had given birth before it arrived. When the ambulance finally arrived, the staff helped the wife and their newborn into the ambulance and gave a loaner car to her husband to get to the hospital. The dealership's staff made sure that the Lexus car that was driven by the couple was completely detailed back to the original condition, and provided a full tank of gas. A few days later, the new family came back to the dealership to retrieve the car. They were greatly surprised and very appreciative towards the staff at the dealership. To show their gratitude for the kindness of the staff, the couple chose "Alexus" as the middle name of their newborn child and invited the staff to her 1st birthday party. Local newspapers and media were there to cover the party as a feel-good story for the general public.

Sales do not always follow a certain manual. We must not always only follow our manuals, but also be creative with our own improvement ideas so that quality of our customer service continues to be enhanced. Our customers are always the stars of a Lexus story. It is our obligation to assist each of our customers to maintain their quality of life by providing excellent services and products. Therefore, each employee in our sales and marketing department has to put themselves in our customers' shoes and remain responsive to their requests and concerns. Overall, every dealership was highly motivated and was capable of solving problems by themselves, avoiding any fundamental issues and a requirement for us to intervene. We have always made sure that our network of dealerships consisted of only those dealerships that are able to do just that.

In general, our contract with Toyota dealerships is renewed every six years. However, dealerships that are below the Lexus standards are required to renew their contracts every two years under the condition that they will continuously improve their quality of service. The criteria for their evaluation process are based on the volume of sales, the level of customer satisfaction and the quality of their facilities. In particular, we introduced a program called "Elite of Lexus", which enabled us to pay the greatest attention to maintaining a dealership network consisted of only those with excellent records.

A Classic Sense of Luxury

As a conclusion to this chapter, I will describe the ideal sense of luxury that Lexus aspires to provide its customers. When we launched the Lexus brand, we stood on the doctrine of "The Relentless Pursuit of Perfection." The sense of luxury that has been accumulated in the past will not be sufficient; relying on the past will make us fall behind the times. In fact, the mission given to Lexus as the "premium brand" must be future-minded and keep searching for the "evolving sense of luxury." This is indeed the Toyota Way that seeks continuous improvement while never becoming satisfied with current conditions.

Our earliest Lexus model, the LS 400, achieved a fuel efficiency of 23 miles per gallon and was the first in the luxury-car category to avoid the Gas Guzzler Tax. That tax was imposed upon US domestic sale of new vehicles that did not meet certain fuel standards set by the US Environmental Protection Agency in order to

THE TOYOTA WAY IN SALES & MARKETING

achieve energy consumption reductions and improve the quality of the environment. As for the interior of the LS 400 model, the dashboard was equipped with advanced gauges and a TV screen with state-of-the-art sound system. It was also designed to provide customers with a "healing environment" by fine-tuning the sound of closing doors and simulating that unique smell of a brand new car. Building these enhancements into the products and services will always accomplish a level of luxury that will always be one step ahead of general expectations.

A Lexus that is technologically advanced, and identifies itself with a great deal of finesse, promises to provide customer with the best quality experience by assuring a sense of "excitement" and "elegance." Although it maybe said that the feelings of "excitement" and "elegance" cannot be accomplished simultaneously, we strongly believe that it is possible for Lexus to do so because Lexus analyzes and incorporates critical specifications derived from many different perspectives, with much higher expectations.

As a revolutionary brand, "Lexus" continues to attract customers with innovative designs and high value in "customer hospitality" and has earned great recognition with the public. Steven Spielberg directed a film titled *Minority Report* that included his version of what Lexus would look like in 2054. Lexus cars have also appeared in a popular novel written by Dan Brown titled *The Da Vinci Code* and many others by my favorite writer, John Grisham. Lexus cars are loved and integrated into the lives of people all over the world. In this sense, Lexus cars are the proof for having fully embodied the visions and missions that were defined in the Toyota Way in Sales and Marketing.

By the way, the word "Lexus" was derived from a German word "Luxus," meaning "luxury" and "first-class" and was selected among other 216 suggestions after a series of discussions. I suspect that one of the deciding factors was the "L" and "X" sound that were crisp and clear to our ears.

CHAPTER 5

OUR MINDSET BEHIND SALES AND MARKETING

The Toyota Way as I See It

As I explained in the previous chapters, the Toyota Way does not follow a certain set of routines. The important thing is to comply with the common rules of the Toyota Way. However, each person must actively seek a "My Way" in the realm of the Toyota Way by utilizing his own ideas and techniques to be built on the basic principles defined in the Toyota Way. Eventually, this attitude leads to the true Toyota Way.

I had my own unique way as well. When I moved on from the executive vice president position in 2005, I was asked to write about it. Then, I decided to publish a booklet named *Yoshi's 8 Rules* that included my techniques along with lecture topics and presentation materials I used in the past. My eight rules are one of the many Toyota Way examples known to exist. Many employees will find them a useful tool to present practical applications of the Toyota Way in Sales and Marketing. Please look at the following chart.

Yoshi's 8 Rules

1. Have an open mind and love of travel
2. Be a good listener
3. Pack a positive attitude
4. Be healthy in mind and body
5. Be a student for life
6. Respect others
7. Build the entire team
8. Have fun!

Figure 45: Yoshi's Eight Rules

These rules are not promoting a high level of philosophy or technologies at all. Even though these rules seem to be a basic and simple mindset, they are important factors that I became acutely aware of through my experiences in working overseas in the USA and Australia, and managing business all over the world.

Life is Not all About Work

I would like to first emphasize the importance of making your work enjoyable. So, I will explain my eighth rule, "Have fun!" My philosophy is that life is too short to devote to just working. In other words, your job never deserves to have full control over your life.

Can you imagine how much fun your work would be if you brought your personal life into it?

I am against the idea that only business-related topics are to be discussed in a business meeting. It should be perfectly acceptable to either start a conversation about personal interests, or go explore the local community with business partners in a foreign country. Find time to tackle new sports and walk into the wilderness to see some wild animals. Human beings have a tendency to remember more vividly those moments where our personalities are revealed, and people who show interests in others surely know how to have fun with their lives. I often ask about people's hobbies. This is how I seek connections with other people to have a quality time together and talking about hobbies is always extremely effective for me. When I have a meeting with my subordinates, I ask them between discussions,

"By the way, what are your hobbies?"

One of the subordinates answered, "Skiing. I love going to the resort city of Yuzawa in winter for some skiing fun. "

I kept his answer in the back of my head and asked him when I ran into him in the bathroom some days later,

"How is Yuzawa this season? Is it getting enough snow this year?"

My subordinates usually act surprised when I ask them follow-up questions like this one. They will later develop an appreciation toward me for remembering small facts about their personal lives; this is our connection I am taking about here. The same is true for Americans. Most of them enjoy more hobbies than the Japanese and it keeps me curious to learn by actively sharing their experiences in activities such as biking and hiking. It is a remarkable idea to enjoy hobbies as much as you can because they can clearly separate your work from your personal life. Forget about your work on weekends and immerse yourself in your hobbies. This is the most effective way to prepare workers for the following week of work.

Figure 46: The Importance of Free Time & Leisure Activities

How to Switch Your Mind to Weekend Mode

One of my techniques that I used with my subordinates for many years was to have them create a To-Do list every Friday before they left the office for the weekend. Workers would list up all of their pending jobs on a piece of paper and stick the list on their desks. Then I would tell them, "Alright! Good job! Your work for this week is over," and encouraged them to switch their minds to a weekend-mode. The most important thing is to make sure that workers do not take their work home to be completed over the weekend. Have them enjoy their Saturdays and Sundays off at leisure to the fullest while forgetting about their work completely. Have them come to work on Monday with a refreshed mind and start going down their list to complete the pending jobs. This allows workers to maintain a high level of productivity, especially on gloomy Mondays.

I came up with this method when I was the chief representative in Australia. Despite my title, our office was occupied only by me and my secretary, having to perform a large amount of work on a daily basis. I started making a To-Do list so I would not forget over the weekend, which made me feel relieved and allowed me to become more productive, so I continued. After putting away my list in the drawer, I left the office to find beautiful Sydney Bay in front of my eyes. I often spent my evenings fishing on a dock after work. Sometimes, I would go fishing on Saturdays and Sundays and become so consumed in it that the day passed quickly.

Through my off-duty fishing experiences, I have become acquainted with many other fishing enthusiasts and developed a unique network of friendships outside of my work. It was such a meaningful way to spend my weekends. As well, I had many weekends where I was so engaged in reading that I lost track of time on weekends. When I lived in Australia, I read every single work by Frederick Forsyth. When I lived in the US, I started reading the original texts in English. Especially, I became a huge fan of John Grisham and could hardly wait for his new books to be published. Reading my favorite books by Grisham such as *A Time to Kill*, *The Firm*, and *The Testament*, literally made me forget about time and helped me care the least about my work. Many of Grisham's popular books have been made into box-office movies, which often came up as a good conversation topic between my coworkers and me. In some cases, my coworkers gave me Grisham's new books in a situation such as this one,

"Yoshi, you know about Grisham's new book that just came out? You're a big fan, aren't you?"

"Really? That's news to me. I need to buy one soon."

"Don't worry about buying it now. Take mine with you, I finished reading it."

As I illustrated with my experiences, it is extremely important to get into a habit of "not bringing work home." This may be difficult to carry out in Japanese workplaces where overtime is commonly accepted among workers, even at Toyota. In recent years, workers were not permitted to take computers outside their office mainly for protecting the privacy of critical corporate data. How about we take advantage of this change in policy of modern corporations, and stop bringing work into your personal life for a change?

A Healthy Mind and Body Make a Successful Business Person

My fourth rule, "Be healthy in mind and body" is an essential requirement for becoming a successful business person. I am sure that you have experienced how even the slightest trouble either with your mind or body affects your work performance in many ways. The important thing is to maintain a balance in life and control your eating habits, sleeping, recreation and exercise so that your mind and body will always stay in shape. Although it is important to be social and participate in casual corporate gatherings, I made it a rule to avoid going to fancy and excessively formal dinner parties and, when I have to attend a banquet to serve my role, I always leave early. When I was an executive vice-president for Toyota in Japan, I would often go on business trips that required me to fly round-trip from Japan to foreign countries more than twenty times a year. Many people take some sleeping pills to avoid jet lag. But, I have always chosen to take none for myself because I dislike the way they affected the balance of my life, which I carefully maintain on a daily basis.

Figure 47: Remembering What is Important

Spending quality time with my family was also indispensable for me to lead a healthy life. Especially on foreign soil where we were not accustomed to many things, I often found myself reconfirming my family bonds and felt a much stronger sense of compassion toward my family, and I received the same from my wife and children in return. I dedicate my long and successful career entirely to my family; I simply could not have done it without them. The most fundamental and significant entity in any society is the family unit. The meaning of your life and your professional role can be greatly enhanced by cherishing this fundamental principle of family-values.

Travel with an Open Mind

Nowadays, the world is getting smaller with the help of information technology. This enables each professional to visit anywhere in the world in order to accumulate a great deal of hands-on experiences. The first rule, "Have an open mind and love of travel" must be kept in the minds of not only expatriate officers as I once was, but also of any business person in our modern society.

It was in 1975 when I started my residence in Australia. It was my 12th year into my career at Toyota. For the early period of my stay, I would feel nostalgic about Japan and would share some local Japanese news with my family members, saying something like "The neighborhood we used to live in just had a fire. How sad…" I also liked mingling with local Australians; I would try my hardest to get as much local information as possible from those I met for work. When someone told me that there was a car accident nearby, I always expand the conversation by asking for details with questions like, "Which intersection did the accident occur at?" or "How is speeding regulated by the police around here?" Some local people also gave me some useful information about seasonal events and points of interests that many people were simply unaware of. I was acting like a journalist and collected exclusive information for the best local spots for my favorite activities including visiting the ocean, barbecues, and golfing. As I put my collected information to the test with my family, I began absorbing many positive things about the local community and acknowledged Sydney as my second home town after six months of living there. As I read about the world weather forecasts on a newspaper, I found myself checking the weather in Sydney rather than that in Tokyo, as I had always done at the early part of my residency in Australia.

Human beings continue to change once they become familiarized with a new environment. The first thing to do in living in a strange land is to be open-minded and try to enjoy what it has to offer as much as possible. By doing so, you will develop a sense of attachment and belonging to the local community, which eventually creates a relationship between you and the local people. Without building such a foundation, the true work cannot be done leaving things unfinished. As for a language barrier, it is not as big a deal as we think it is. I was not a good

English speaker upon my arrival, however, living in Australia for six years helped me become proficient at speaking English. The secret is to practice the language rather than hitting text books. I used to keep the radio turned on during my 1-hour commute to work in order to have my ears accustomed to the sounds of English language. My next step was to try it out in a conversation without worrying about grammatical errors. Listen and speak as much as you possibly can. If you repeatedly do that, I guarantee that you will automatically become good at speaking English.

Positive Results are Always Attainable if You Follow the Rules

Toyota began its full-fledged expansion to Australia in the 60s, prior to advancing into the US and European markets. It was a period when product models such as Land Cruiser, Corolla, and our pickup truck named "Hilux" were selling extremely well in the Australian market. One of the reasons Toyota got into the Australian market so fast was that Toyota could only export their passenger cars by the "Complete Knock Down" production method, which required automakers to transport individual components first and perform the final assembly in Australia. In addition, regulations that favored domestically-produced products became a statutory requirement for automakers, which required Toyota to manufacture and procure many components in Australia. Consequently, Toyota built a factory in Melbourne where passenger cars are manufactured with high local content, i.e., internally made parts and outsourced components.

What Toyota had gone through in Australia provided a perfect learning opportunity for Toyota's subsequent advances into the US and European markets. The production department learned effective ways of manufacturing that was in accordance with the local requirements. On the other hand, the sales and marketing department learned how to analyze the market needs by studying the local environment and gained an understanding from our presence amongst the local people by effectively showing our commitment through our sales network.

At that time, we did not have fax machines so I was responsible for writing up reports to be mailed to the headquarters in Japan. My report included summaries of the "Voice of the Locals" where I had carefully analyzed the feedback collected from sales network on the frontline. In addition, I held product planning meetings once a year with managers from the overseas planning and development department from headquarters. I presented my requests in the meetings by saying,

> "Can you engineer a car with these specific specifications and produce this type of a product line?"

In other words, my requests were targeted to specific details like:

> "Can you increase the capacity of the engine?"
> or "Is it possible to stick with 5-speed transmission system since our competitors are strong on that?"

The fact that we always reflected customer's needs into our products in this manner has always contributed to the tremendous success of Toyota.

Of course, there have been many incidents where things did not go as planned in some of the countries where Toyota attempted to gain ground. However, the most important thing is to put your ideas in practice first by visiting the actual places while staying open-minded with an inquisitive mind. Then, follow the process by analyzing the current situation and exercising your ingenuity in formulating new solutions. If you followed this rule it would be worth your time and effort even when something went wrong. What you gain in this process will be extremely useful to you in overcoming future challenges with confidence.

The Era of Inclusive Leadership

It has often been said that the Japanese are generally uncomfortable in expressing their honest opinions and emotions. I agree with that and also believe that Japanese are bad listeners as well. Fundamentally speaking, listening and speaking skills go hand in hand to establish a good communication skill. Your appropriate reactions must be demonstrated to others by showing your genuine interest in the topics being discussed during a conversation. Instead of just nodding your head, stay engaged in the conversation by expressively showing your agreement or reinforcing other's opinions, by providing them with supportive information that you may have to add. You can also argue with others in a conversation by showing your disagreement based on your own theories. These techniques allow you to convey your reactions in a comprehensive manner to others and establish effective two-way communications. In other words, effective communications cannot be established if one party remains passive either in listening or speaking. In this sense, bad listeners and bad speakers can always coexist.

Rule number two, "Be a good listener," is essentially a doctrine for all of us to become supportive listeners as it is the foundation for maintaining effective communications. If you pay closer attention to every word you hear, you will begin to read the minds of others and understand the true intention that they are attempting to convey. This is extremely useful as others are sometimes discouraged to voluntarily express their purposes in a straight-forward manner. Also, your attitude shows your honest interest in attempting to acknowledge other's objectives. This creates a great influence upon others to become open-minded in return.

It is a requirement for any person in a leadership role to have the ability to listen to others carefully. If a leader begins to force his opinions or conclusions upon others before any opportunity is given for others to respond, it would simply be the same as a transmission of information, and would neither establish a sense of togetherness, nor a collective responsive reaction in the minds of the listeners. I am adamant about teamwork and development of each worker. These are the fruits of the clearly defined process that incorporates sharing ideas and allowing debate for finding better solutions in order to converge every participating individual into the same direction. I call this process "inclusive management" (management with full participation).

Figure 48: Being A Good Listener

©Toyota Motor Corporation
Used with permission. Permission does not imply endorsement.

A business magazine titled *Strategy & Business*, published by prominent international consulting company Booz Allen Hamilton Inc., included an article entitled "CEO Succession 2006: The Era of the Inclusive Leader" in the summer issue of 2007. The article presented an analysis of research based upon a survey of 2,500 major publicly traded corporations. It found that many modern companies have encouraged the adoption of a management style where the leadership plays a significant role in providing group guidance while demanding participation from each individual worker, as opposed to a decision making process that relies on a charismatic individual to forcibly push the entire company in the direction they see fit.

I personally have made a great deal of effort to be a good listener and internalized opinions that I determined to be beneficial. When I was the president of Toyota Motor Sales, U.S.A., Inc., I used to enjoy having small talks with my designated driver. Once in a while, he told me some interesting stories. I would immediately tell him, "Wow, what an interesting perspective. I should definitely try it!" and discussed his unique ideas and explored their legitimacy in a corporate meeting. Such an inclusive management technique that I implemented is bound to enhance the motivation and loyalty of every single employee — including my driver — towards Toyota as a whole.

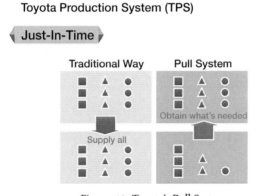

Figure 49: Toyota's Pull System

Listen to the Market

I sometimes describe "Be a good listener" with another interpretation as "Be sure to listen to the market." True work cannot be continued unless we comprehensively know what kind of car customers are wishing for, as well as their expectation toward Toyota itself. I assure you that Toyota has carefully listened to the voices of dealers and distributors and made it a priority to gain collective support, as I have described in this book so far. Professionally speaking, Toyota has embedded it-self in the "Market-in" philosophy which allowed Toyota to supply only the right products in the right quantity at the right time based on the analysis of needs and expectations of the cus-tomers. Toyota still continues to practice this "Pull System" in the realm of sales and marketing.

On the other hand, the big 3 automakers of the US had oper-ated by following marketing strategies that they believed to be the best only for themselves for a long time. It was only in recent years when they began paying much closer attention to market changes, and learned to implement necessary adjustments in production such as controlling the volume of inventory and re-ducing the production volume of unpopular cars.

However, in the past, they heavily promoted a "Push System" in sales and marketing, which commanded dealerships to sell off a certain number of cars based on the total volume of production output. Having learned from the experiences of these US auto-makers, it is true to attribute Toyota's long-term success to our carefully designed sales and marketing techniques which opted for a completely different approach.

In order to effectively research the market needs, the methods we use must be diverse and carried out in a multilateral manner. For example, the development of a new car requires an analysis of the targeted customers' lifestyles by conducting a survey of their current living conditions. As I explained in the previous chapter on Lexus, the design and engineering of an ideal car is to be conceptualized first by learning every fact about customers' lives. This includes the type of housing they live in and favorite interior designs, so that the new car can be easily adapted into their existing living styles.

After the completion of a new car, we organize an important event called a "Product Clinic" where a sample of targeted cus-tomers are invited to provide us with constructive feedbacks and test for any inconvenience prior to the official market launch. In some instances, we hid the Toyota logo on the cars to be tested and had what we called a "masked clinic" in different parts of the US. Our purpose was to eliminate any biases that our customers may have had towards different brands and create an environment where they could provide us with

Figure 50: Toyota Product Clinic

©Toyota Motor Corporation
Used with permission. Permission does not
imply endorsement.

their honest opinions that were to be carefully incorporated into improving the quality of our products by our Research and Development department. In addition, we carry out many other diverse types of post-release research according to the nature of our interests and objectives. For example, a market research called "Early Bird" is taking place to study the actual usability of our newly-launched cars.

Marketing and Production Are Two Different Things

When I was working in Australia I began seriously studying many different marketing techniques in general. Looking back on the last sixty years, the market has evolved through several phases. The period from the end of World War II up to 1960s could be called the era of supply shortage, from the 60's to the 70'the "Era of Production" and the period of the rapid economic growth between 1970s through the middle of 1980's the "Era of Sales". The period from the middle of 1980s when an overwhelming amount of available products had to be differentiated can be referred as the "Era of Marketing." I was in Australia from 1975 to 1981 when the "Era of Marketing" was about to draw a curtain aside to the global market. These phases serve to illustrate that as times change, so does the business environment.

What surprised me the most was the fact that in Australia, sales people leisurely waited for customers to come into the dealership throughout the day. At the same time, sales people in Japan marketed their new cars mainly by their door-to-door selling methods. They would go around in a neighborhood with a local reference map in their hands and visit the house of each potential customer to be persuaded into purchasing. On the other hand, sales people in Australia often said, "Our responsibility is to sell customers who are already in our showrooms. However, it is a responsibility of automakers and our dealership managers to entice people into coming to our dealerships."

One of the factors that can explain the different attitudes towards marketing tactics between Australian and Japanese sales people is the fact that each country has its own unique peculiarities. Door-to-door marketing activities would be next to impossible in Australia with the total continental area of 7.7 million sq km, which is more than 20 times larger than Japan. On the other hand, one of the intentions behind the Japanese door-to-door marketing practices was to research the financial viability of potential buyers. Trusting customer's financial stability was a big challenge for Japanese companies back then due to the lack of systems designed to check customer's credit background. The only way for Japanese sales people to establish the viability of potential customers was to assess on location the physical condition of customers' assets, such as housing.

Another factor is that Australian businesses have accumulated a great deal of marketing knowledge and already established effective ways of reaching customers in their unique environment. They have conducted scientific marketing research that indicated the most productive marketing techniques utilized different media formats such as radio and television, and helped them learn the most appropriate timing for releasing advertisements and how to articulate their sales pitches for each type of media. Luckily, I was able to learn this information and found it extremely beneficial to my own marketing endeavors.

That said, staff at Toyota's production department often said to me in the past, "We have been visiting overseas to teach the Toyota Production System to local factories. The sales department should do the same. Why not send some of your competent sales experts abroad to spread the Toyota Way in Sales and Marketing?" However, I have personally recognized that our direct knowledge of sales and marketing peculiar to Japan could not be transferred to businesses to other countries so easily. An appropriate method was to match the unique state of affairs existing in each country and to listen to the voices from the target market to determine the appropriate marketing approach.

Toyota at the present time has regional headquarters in the US, Europe (Belgium) and Asia & Oceania (Singapore), staffed with specialists whose purpose is to provide Toyota with national and regional information that is essential for customizing various marketing materials prepared by Toyota. These offices are under the strict supervision of the global marketing division at headquarters which, in turn, supplies the necessary marketing information, such as product catalogues and manuals, as well as basic resources for creating advertisement. However, it is entirely up to the regional headquarters to decide how the information should be arranged and which marketing strategies are most effective and relevant by judging the unique market characteristics of each community. For example, for publishing an advertisement for a new car, the headquarters provides regional headquarters with various background data targeted for marketing and includes information such as specification comparison charts, instruction manuals and videos and photos taken from every angle. Then, the regional offices are given freedom to pick information they believe to be fitting best and continue to compile the final advertisement one after another according to the needs of the local market.

Automobile Culture of Japan, the United States, & Europe

People's expectations towards automobiles vary greatly depending upon the country and region of the world. Needless to say, automobiles are being utilized for a wide range of purposes that have strong connections with each nation's historical background and geographical characteristics, as well as the unique characteristics of local residents. With this in mind, Toyota sends a Research and Development study team to the targeted country or specific region in order to perform background research prior to developing a new car. The team analyzes in detail from the life style of the customers to the condition of local street infrastructures and observes how automobiles are being operated by local drivers. This information allows the team to engineer to best match the blueprint for the new car including many fitting attributes like design, style, engine capacity, suspension, interior, etc.

Figure 51: Analyzing the Needs of Customers

©Toyota Motor Corporation
Used with permission. Permission does not imply endorsement.

I can explain this better by looking at each distinctive automobile culture found in Japan, the US, and Europe. In Japan, as all of my Japanese readers already know, small-sized vehicles are the highest in popularity and are commonly used by Japanese since roads are generally narrower due to the size of the country. On the other hand, in much larger countries like the US, Americans have a strong tendency to stick with large-size vehicles with large engine capacity and enjoy driving around in a laid-back manner. In Europe, with a long automobile history for more than 100 years, people have their preference on high-performance cars that are also compact in size and stylish in their eyes. Despite the fact that I have never had an opportunity to work in Europe, I held a seat at the Japanese headquarters and was assigned a responsibility of managing the European market for about seven years. I learned then how to effectively manage and respond to the diversity within that market. Calling the entire region "Europe" simply does not do justice as it consists of many different countries that proudly honor their distinctive languages and cultures.

The same is true when it comes to deciding what kind of automobiles is the best-fit for the European market. Product development meetings always produced varying opinions and expectation from representatives of each of the European countries. For example, representatives often have a disagreement on mundane issues such as body colors like "red, yellow or black", which I found to be quite trivial. In this type of situation, we needed to expand our targeted sample areas and engage in repeated conversations with local distributors so that we could make sure our final decision was based upon as many inputs as possible from the local market.

Furthermore, each country has its own peak sales seasons. In Europe that peak is usually in spring and fall. However, sales peaked in August for the United Kingdom in the past due to switching of the license plates (these days license switch happens in March and September), and a sales peak is reached in January in Ireland and Finland.

Every factor in a business environment is influenced by the unique sales trends and tax systems of each country and must be taken into consideration for formulating our marketing mechanisms and finding the most effective way to manage inventory based on demand. In order to accomplish this, instead of forcing instructions from the Japanese headquarters, we built our regional headquarters so that the market needs could be regionally addressed and analyzed in the process of building our marketing policies. As a result, the main regional headquarters for our European market is located now in Belgium allowing us to closely monitor the changing demand of the various European countries. Consequently, Toyota's market share for the European region has drastically increased from only 2% at the time to approximately 6.5% in 2006.

Designs that Meet Regional Characteristics and the Modernization of Our Time

In the US, also known as the land of opportunity and freedom, the market possesses a great inclination to highly evaluate products on the basis of the quality and actual value of a product. In the European market, where nationalistic traditions and history are highly respected, the market has a tendency to assess the quality of a product by supplemental values in order to make sure that a product clearly represents the deep-rooted European identity, ideologies and creativity, especially from a "fashionable" perspective. The main reason Toyota had a difficult time being accepted by European consumers was because Toyota was considered to be an immature automaker compared to the local automakers such as BMW, Mercedes, and Renault with well-established recognition and history. Toyota also had to face a challenge of eliminating a common assumption that not only Toyota, but also all other Japanese-made cars were made with "very poor" designs and interior furnishings. Toyota spent a tremendous amount of time just to make people appreciate and believe just the opposite.

In 1999, the introduction of the "Yaris" model (also known as "Vitz" in Japan) into the European small-car market as part of a battle plan brought a huge breakthrough to Toyota. Yaris, having an exceptional performance for its size and comfortable interior space by an innovative design, experienced explosive sales and turned the Toyota image completely around with European consumers. That adorable design of Yaris was a work of art by a Greek designer from a design studio located in the south of France.

Figure 52: The Toyota Yaris

©Toyota Motor Corporation
Used with permission. Permission does not imply endorsement.

Toyota built three global design institutes in Japan, the US (California) and Europe (South of France), which allow local designers to experiment with their unique ideas and test their intuition in order to meet the objectives set for each region.

Besides paying close attention to the unique characteristics of the local market, the global design studios continue to create innovative designs that reflect the modernization of our time. Two types of designs are being conceptualized. One is called "Commercial Design" targeted for the next-generation cars to appear on the market. The other is called "Imaginary Design" that helps us visualize what our cars ought to look like 10 years ahead. As you have noticed, different types of fashion and music come and go, automobile designs also experience a series of fads over time. For example, a cubic body design can be in style for a certain period of time and later changes to a circular design just to retain popularity. I sometimes thought that our creative designs may have been a bit too far-fetched at the time of creation. However, I was able to look at the same design 10 years later without any feeling of strangeness. I am very proud of our designers being able to look into the future.

There was a time when people even outside Europe thought that Toyota cars became less appealing as they became so close to perfection. In other words, even though Toyota cars had proven their excellence in terms of Quality, Dependability, and Reliability (QDR), people had a cynical view criticizing Toyota for lacking uniqueness in automobile style and design. However, in recent years, based on these comments, we closely listened to the voice of our markets and incorporated globally-favored designs into our products which has successfully eliminated such criticism of "being too stodgy."

Emphasizing "Respect for People" is the Foundation for Human Relationships

Claims from customers vary significantly according to which country or region claims are being voiced. For example, in Japan, drivers honk the horn only when they absolutely need to. However, drivers in Southeast Asia often blow the horn more than they should, which often leads to customer claims due to worn-out klaxon components. The quality of gasoline used across the world must also be taken into our consideration. Some countries sell separate types of gasoline for summer and winter using special additives. If we failed to analyze what is exactly in the gasoline supplied in each country, problems causing a fuel clog in the engine would be inevitable and lead to claims.

Our customer call centers play a vital role in giving us an opportunity to learn, first hand, every detail of customer concerns and demands. I consider our customer call centers to be excellent antennas for receiving critical information. When a problem is reported by a certain customer and continues to get reported by many other affected customers, we immediately initiate a technical advisory meeting to find the most effective solution to the problem by running a series of experiments on the actual model in question. When a recall is needed, our customer sales records are searched to narrow down who the affected customers are. Each of these customers is contacted and the necessary repairs are arranged. The most important thing to remember in conducting a recall is to secure the necessary components and carry out the repairs in a timely fashion without making customers wait at all. As I already explained in the previous chapter on Lexus, appropriate handling of customer claims and treating customers in an efficient and timely manner in the case of a recall are extremely critical in developing and sustaining a strong trusting relationship with customers.

These days, the construction of a single automobile requires more electronic components than the number of components that were originally needed to build the rocket for landing on the moon. This means that most of the defects found these days are becoming computer-related issues, which makes it much more complicated and challenging for us to analyze the true cause and develop an appropriate solution. Therefore, responding to customer's claims with a greater level of urgency and sincerity provides us with much useful guidance towards overcoming potential challenges in the future. We must also remember that the way we handle customer's claims is like a litmus test that clearly shows how much respect and care we are really giving to customers.

What does it really mean to highly value and respect people?

I believe that it is to be as thoughtful as you possibly can towards other people. It also means to create abundant opportunities for you to look at things from the perspectives of those around you. Showing a respectful attitude towards others is the most crucial factor in establishing meaningful human relationships. Activities such as listening closely to the market, being open-minded and following the local customs continue to show our profound respect for those living in different areas of the world. Gathering the voices of our marketing representatives working on the front line is another indication of paying respect. Sales representatives maintain the closest proximity to our valued customers and are equipped with a proven capacity to make the right judgments. They certainly deserve every drop of our respect, in my opinion. I cannot stress enough that the most important thing is to listen carefully to what others have to say with the highest consideration and without concern about whose opinions are right or wrong. This alone is exactly what I mean by my sixth rule, "Respect others."

Secrets to Evoke a Revolution

One step beyond "Respect" is the relationship of "Trust"; a solid trusting relationship brings people even closer and creates a much stronger spirit of collective teamwork. In order to follow my seventh rule, "Build the entire team," leaders must first win the trust of every player on the team. What I have always made sure to practice over the years was to model to my team, through actual examples, the appropriate behavior and management practices at the forefront as much as possible. Whenever I was in a meeting or on a business trip with my subordinates, I would never step back and leave everything up to them, but instead took a proactive role by saying "Look at how I solve this problem. If I explained everything in words, it would take forever. Just stay beside me and take notes." A picture is worth a thousand words. By showing how a real job is performed in front of their eyes, young and inexperienced staff become capable of understanding each situation in their own way. They can also effectively pick up from my real experiences some useful know-how in communicating with others required for the many different situations they will encounter, such as completing difficult business negotiations, expressing opinions including those that are of a delicate manner, and turning down unsound business offers without offending anyone. Consequently, my subordinates often began to show their positive attitudes by telling me, "I completely get it now and thank you for giving me this learning opportunity. Please allow me to handle the case from now on."

I have also made sure to put as much effort as I could to maintain close communication toward those that were under adverse conditions and corporate divisions whose opinions were usually ignored. When I became the president of Toyota Motor Sales, U.S.A., Inc., in 1996, I made myself available more than ever before to interact with staff from departments other than the sales and marketing division, such as legal, logistics, information technology, administration, human resources and accounting. I would ask, "What can we do to improve our company? I am dying to have each one of you to share your ideas with me." There was a downside to this too. Staff from the marketing department often told me, "Please pay more attention to your own department. We all came to depend on you as the president because of your strong background in sales and marketing. How come you're more involved in talking to other departments?" I totally understood their frustration as Toyota Motor Sales, U.S.A., Inc. was essentially a sales company.

However, it is true to say that Toyota Motor Sales, U.S.A., Inc., being a sales-oriented institution, had high employee standards — especially for its sales and marketing division. As a matter of fact, my subordinates held excellent records of accomplishment at all times and were simply natural at performing sales and marketing. I still consider myself nothing but a sales person from the beginning. Visiting some dealerships briefly and skimming through sales records and marketing documents was always sufficient for me to get a bigger picture, as far as the status of my division was concerned.

My point is that I did make a clear decision to deliberately pay closer attention to departments other than sales and marketing, while taking into consideration the balance within the entire company so that the level of motivation among employees could be enhanced as a whole. I strongly believe that Employee Satisfaction (ES) has to be strengthened to a great degree in order to cultivate a better Customer Satisfaction (CS). In other words, our customers would not be fully satisfied unless every single employee of ours was fully content with their working environment and was excited to perform their responsibilities.

Being the President Made Me Realize the Existence of "Big Corporate Disease" within Toyota

As I gathered opinions from the staff working in various management sectors of Toyota, what I heard from them was often refreshing to someone like me who had always been a marketing-oriented executive. For example, marketing people like me concentrate only on considering ways to sell as much as possible. At the same time, we often lack motivation to attempt to save internal costs in the daily work routine. However, I noticed that staff in administration divisions were trying everything they possibly could to reduce the cost of printable papers even by 10 Yen per 10,000 sheets. I fully encouraged my staff to suggest their idea to me, such as, "If we decide to use a lower-quality paper for printing, we will be able to reduce our cost by 10 Yen per 10,000 sheets. Since we use this paper for internal documents, I think we can compromise on the quality of paper." I would respond to such a person by saying, "Please continue to think about similar continuous improvement ideas no matter how small they may be."

I went beyond talking only to my employees at headquarters and continued to visit other related facilities to hear more voices. I am going to share my experience when I visited a maintenance facility in Long Beach, California where the final inspection was being performed prior to shipment to our dealers. After inspecting the facility, I discovered a process in which technicians were lying on their backs to perform their jobs. They later told me that they were in charge of attaching a wiring harness to the air-conditioning unit on the bottom of each car. They also express their concern by saying, "This particular job requires us to lie on our back all day long. In fact, many of us are suffering a severe backache from it. Is there any better way for us to perform the task?" I immediately gathered up executives in related fields and reached an agreement that every single process had to be reviewed and ergonomically comfortable. In this particular case, we did exactly that while studying the actual car in question and achieved a series of continuous improvements.

When I visited warehouses for storing our components in Ohio, I could not believe what I saw there. None of the presidents in the history of Toyota Motor Sales, U.S.A., Inc., had a desire to come and inspect a warehouse in the past, which was reason enough alone for me to visit. A local manager guided me to see only the four out of six warehouses that we were renting locally. He unlocked the doors to the four warehouses while keeping the other two warehouses securely locked. I finally asked him,

"Why are you keeping me from those two warehouses? What is in them?"

The manager replied, "Well sir, you have already seen four warehouses. Those remaining warehouses store the same components as others. You would not be interested."

I replied, "I came this far to see everything. Go ahead and open them."

The manager reluctantly allowed me inside the remaining warehouses. What I saw inside was a pile of jewelry accessories that we had ordered from a vendor to be used for some product campaign in the past. In other words, it had become dead stock for many years without any scheduled release date. I was surprised to find out the amount of money we had been spending so far in order to keep these warehouses. The manager told me that it had cost Toyota the total amount of six million US dollars just to keep this dead stock without adding any value whatsoever to our operations. I immediately ordered the manager to empty the warehouse out after disposing the dead stock completely, and analyzed why this nonsense had come about in the first place.

Later I discovered the true cause to be a lack of horizontal coordination among the departments within our company. My investigation revealed that the component department designed and manufactured the promotional jewelry accessories after projecting a release date of the special campaign planned by the marketing department. However, they ended up storing it in the warehouse only to find out that the model was no longer scheduled to be released, leaving the promotional jewelry accessories to become a huge waste. It was basically a typical error caused by the insufficient horizontal communication between two different departments. None of this would have happened if the component department had worked closely together in coordination with the marketing department in charge of the special model. I call this whole incident a typical example of a "big company disease" within Toyota. I admit that the Toyota Motor Sales, U.S.A., Inc. had a bit too much self-confidence and a lukewarm feeling towards its internal organization structure due to the tremendous success of Lexus. At the same time as the organization continued to grow bigger, I felt that the coordination among departments turned rusty due to the vertically segmented administrative system, which significantly slowed down the collective decision making process within the company. I also had an impression that our willingness to take on new challenges diminished because of that lethargy and employees became less enthusiastic about their responsibilities.

Organizational Strength Decides the Outcome of Marketing

Japan experienced a severe market condition in the 1990's when the collapse of a "bubble economy" occurred. In the US as well, the economy went downhill following a substantial increase in oil prices due to the Gulf War accompanied by the strong Japanese currency at the time.

The economic relationship between the US and Japan significantly worsened as seen in the contentious debates that were carried out between the US Trade Representative, Michael Kantor, and Japanese minister of Trade and Industry, Ryutaro Hashimoto in 1995. When I was assigned as the president of Toyota Motor Sales, U.S.A., Inc. in 1996, we found ourselves caught in the middle of such chaos and the economy kept us stagnant for a while. The sales of Lexus remained strong since its brand launch but we failed to meet the sales objective for the first time in 1994 and continued to do so until 1996. I was under a strict order from the headquarters to bring Toyota's US operations back on track by all means. However, I honestly did not think I was up for the challenge and packed only one piece of luggage prior to my departure to the US thinking that I would immediately return if things did not clear up.

To my surprise, my colleagues threw a "morning coffee meeting" on my first day and shook my hand firmly while telling me, "Welcome, Yoshi! We have been dying to have you here. We are all counting on you to revitalize Toyota Motor Sales, U.S.A., Inc." Having seen everyone's expectations towards me, I realized that I could not just give it a try, but had to meet the challenge I was given no matter what it would take.

I created opportunities for sustaining an open communication atmosphere, such as off-site meetings that I described in Chapter 4, and went back to the basics by reviewing with my colleagues what the Toyota Way was all about once again. Examples that I described so far such as consideration towards other administrative departments, continuous improvement performed during the warehouse inspection, and discovery of dead stocks are results of our strong leadership based on the Toyota Way principles of "Elimination of Wastes" (The 3Ms: Muri, Muda and Mura, or Irrationality, Waste, and Variation), and "Genchi-genbutsu."

As I continued to take on the necessary leadership role, I listened to the opinions of others closely. I encountered a number of employees who told me, "President, please allow me to take charge of this matter" and provided me with creative solutions that Japanese employees could not have come up with as Americans have totally different ways of approaching issues in general. An American employee once told me bluntly, "This issue is not a big deal, so don't stress yourself over it and solve it financially. As the saying goes, "Money talks." It is our best solution in terms of cost, money and for avoiding possible lawsuits." The accounting department would automatically react to this type of solution by saying, "It is not up to us. We must get approval from the Japanese headquarters." However, the final decision was entirely up to me as the president. I made it clear that I would take full responsibility and gave his idea a try. I persuaded my colleagues by saying, "Just inform the Japan side that the problem has been solved. In the meanwhile, let us take prompt action and believe in ourselves."

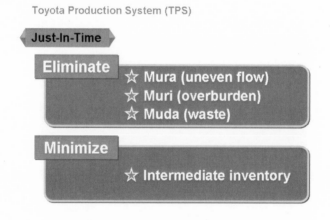

Figure 53: The 3Ms

Ideas from each individual alone have no influence. The final result of our work is greatly dependent on whether ideas from each individual can be assembled together by a leader in order to strengthen the teamwork so that problems can be solved by collective effort. Especially in the field of marketing, I believe that such an organizational strength is the most critical factor in determining who the winner is.

The Threat of Category Killers

In order to create a perfect team I told my employees at Toyota Motor Sales, U.S.A., Inc. to adopt a new corporate strategy, "Growth," "Change," and "Development." Each employee must grow, develop, and change according to the changing times, society, and needs of customers in order for the organizations to succeed. Toyota Motor Sales, U.S.A., Inc., made a strong commitment to function on the basis of the Toyota Way with the principles of, "Growth," "Change," and "Development" as its fundamental philosophy at all times. After reflecting on the "dead stock" incident, in which we lost six million dollars, we made sure that our departments coordinated their decision making processes and worked hand in hand in a horizontal manner. We also implemented a system whereby comprehensive post-sales customer support was provided after shifting away from our incorrect assumption that offering services and production of components were completely different entities. We had to identify and eliminate obstacles in order to improve the performance of the organization and enhance motivation of each of our employees.

An ideal work environment had to be created by removing various negative factors in order to enable our employees to maintain a positive attitude towards their work. Negativity in the workplace spreads like wild fire and must be avoided from the beginning. Even a single negative thought creates a spiral of more negative thoughts and can lead to many excuses. That is the reason why rule number three, "Pack a positive attitude," is so important to all of us. It was my duty to put a stop to the circulation of negativity and engage all aspects of daily duties in a positive manner.

Our employees learned to take on positive attitudes and were given an environment in which they could believe that there was a solution to every problem. With a positive attitude, even a serious crisis can become an opportunity. What happened to Lexus when it confronted its very first recall and how we protected ourselves from category killers emerging from the advancement of Internet technology are both good examples of our positive attitude.

In 1996, only 13 years ago, the Internet was becoming readily available to the world. It was around that time when the "category killers" that started entering the automobile dealership industry began to emerge. In 1995, a firm named, "Autobytel," came into the game. It provided automobile brokerage services for purchasing both new and used cars. All a customer had to do was to browse online and make a simple telephone call to make a purchase of their choice. In the US, a dealership license is required to handle auto sales. However, as long as a brokerage firm maintains a business model in which they yield profits in the form of customer consulting fees rather than directly making the actual sale of a vehicle, a dealership license is technically not required. Customers are able to research the specifications and prices of specific cars online in the comfort of their home and perform various comparisons between other dealerships. Brokerage firms also negotiate for better prices with the dealerships directly so that customers do not have to talk to the dealerships at all. Brokerage firms became extremely popular among consumers for these factors of convenience.

Another new business that came into the auto sales industry was a franchise chain called, "AutoNation," that specialized in used cars. The technique they used was to set up a wide range of used cars on their lots and sell them at extremely reasonable prices. The downside was that all of their prices were final and they were never willing to accept any negotiations for a lower price. A prominent business entrepreneur named Wayne Huizenga created AutoNation. He earned his greatest success through establishing a video rental business with Blockbuster video store locations across the United States. He continued to acquire major automobile dealerships with an overpowering amount of financial resources and dared to solicit Toyota dealerships.

A Positive Mindset that Turned Crisis into Opportunity

The question of whether Toyota and AutoNation ought to form a business affiliation became a huge business controversy and triggered many special television programs that broadcast a number of heated discussions among the top executives from both companies. Some Toyota employees and dealerships had opinions that supported the affiliation and many reports from various research institutes, including the census bureau, also indicated that consumers had a tendency to support the affiliation most of the time. The top executives from the US's big three automakers, GM, Ford, and Chrysler announced their predictions by saying, "Our existing dealerships will soon experience some difficulties with their current business model. They will eventually shift towards a completely new business model just like the one supported by AutoNation."

However, we approached the issue from the standpoint of our customers by asking ourselves, "What do our customers genuinely want?" and reached our conclusion that any business models in which the final responsibility did not lie within our company were bound to run into serious limitations. Automobiles are not a kind of product that terminates our relationship with customers when a purchase becomes finalized. Auto–makers must fulfill their commitment to becoming a credible societal entity by continuously providing the customers with various post-sales services including maintenance and repairs. That is the main reason why extensive networks of our dealerships are required across the US. When our dealers were told about our final decision, they told us that AutoNation was nothing for us to be afraid of. "When a customer tells us that AutoNation is selling the same car for a lower price, we will just offer them a better price."

In other words, our dealerships showed a positive approach to use the AutoNation "One Price" policy as weapon against them. On the other hand, AutoNation grew fed up with our quiet attitude and unwillingness to cooperate to their advantage. Representatives from the company jumped the gun and flew to Japan in order to negotiate directly with Mr. Hiroshi Okuda, the president of Toyota Japan at the time. However, Mr. Okuda simply turned them down by saying, "Everything is in the hands of Toyota Motor Sales, U.S.A., Inc."

After all, in spite of the remarkable advancement of Internet infrastructure, Toyota has successfully maintained a solid and intimate relationship of trust with every single dealership in our network across the US that remains strong and continues to function as it should. In fact, overcoming this controversy created a much stronger bond between Toyota and dealerships, as well as among dealerships themselves. Toyota Motor Sales, U.S.A., Inc., started to regain profits starting in 1997. Even though it was a time of severe economic recession in the US, it was due to Toyota's perfect teamwork and positive attitudes towards overcoming various crises that helped us acquire desirable results consistently.

Become an Antenna for Receiving Information Beyond Your Company

I am going to explain my fifth rule, "Be a student for life," as a conclusion for this chapter. There are so many things to learn from in life. Activities such as reading books, listening to others, and traveling, provides us with opportunities to continuously learn about people and societies in different countries. After all, the Internet is a method of learning that we utilize with a great deal of convenience. However, it remains extremely challenging for us to acquire the true essence of subject matters in which we are most interested.

Despite the fact that I stepped down from the role of president at Toyota Motor Sales, U.S.A., Inc., Rule #5 will remain applicable to my life as long as I live. What I have been challenging myself to do in recent years is to obtain information outside the framework of Toyota and consider how such information can be useful and lead to new ideas for Toyota in return.

For example, let us say that a serious natural catastrophic event were to occur somewhere in the world. We question ourselves, "Should Toyota assist with the recovery on its own or in full coordination with the government and the NPO (Non-Profit Organization)?" I keep my antenna high in the global sky with a great sensitivity to the most critical issues and provide the Toyota management team with useful feedback from which they can base their own decisions. As one of the Japanese representatives for the ABAC (APEC Business Advisory Council) within APEC (Asia-Pacific Economic Cooperation), I made a commitment to set my antenna higher than I did when I was the president of Toyota Motor Sales, U.S.A., Inc. in order to expose myself to a much wider range of information available globally.

Chapter 6

Future of the Toyota Way: Lessons from Giants

Practicing What You Preach: Assignment from the Honorary Chairman, Dr. Shoichiro Toyoda

When I describe one of the most important principles in the Toyota Way, genchi-genbutsu, I often receive questions such as this: "Are any activities of going to the actual place to see the actual item in question used for evaluating the work performance of each employee?" The answer is simply, "No." Following the genchi-genbutsu principle does not influence the salary of employees. However, I admit that our employees sometimes feel obliged to try their hardest as they observe the top executives frequently running around the shop floors to practice the genchi-genbutsu principle themselves.

Figure 54: Chairman Shochiro Toyoda

©Toyota Motor Corporation
Used with permission. Permission does not
imply endorsement.

The honorary Chairman, Dr. Shoichiro Toyoda, is more than 80 years old. Despite his age, he remains extremely healthy and continues to travel around the world. When he visited the headquarters of Toyota Motor Sales, U.S.A., Inc. he told us, "I went to check out some dealerships located in this region of the US only to find out that they were not following the rules... Have you been to that part of the country? Have you seen what they are doing yet?" I had no other choice but to reply," I am sorry, I have not visited them to see the problem. I will visit them next month," and took the comments to heart in order to always follow in his footsteps.

The chairman served as the president of the Japan Association for the 2005 World Exposition and achieved various feats and met various challenges in planning for the Aichi Expo of 2005. He put me in charge of a part of the planning process and told me, "Go around the world and visit each country's relevant governmental authorities to promote our Aichi Expo. Beg if you have to so that more countries will participate." I replied to the chairman, "That is a bit too much to ask. I have the entire Toyota overseas operations to look after." He replied, "Of course, I am aware of that. I want you to help me with the Expo and continue to do the same for Toyota." I followed his order and visited each country's Ministry of Trade and Industry offices, as well as Foreign Ministry officials, while carrying a pile of Expo pamphlets in my arms. The chairman taught us his dynamic philosophy that as Toyota executives, we must not only think about Toyota itself, nor just selling cars, but also show a strong willingness to devote ourselves to activities which bring benefits to the welfare of our society in Japan, as well as the world.

He often reminded me of the importance of being a leader by telling me, "Do not worry about small things too much. High-caliber executives like you should never be concerned only about how much money can be made by selling cars. You must start thinking about how you can contribute to our society from now on."

I am sure that many other Toyota executives serving various departments of Toyota received the same advice from him. A few days after, I had another conversation with the chairman while drinking some coffee. He told me,

"Mr. Ishizaka, as you mostly managed international business affairs throughout your career, are you still involved in any international activities?" I replied, "Yes, I am working my hardest to help APEC (Asia Pacific Economic Cooperation)." He replied back, "It is a very good thing for you to get involved with APEC. However, why not try something bigger, like becoming an executive officer for Organization for Economic Co-operation and Development (OECD)?" Even though I told him that I thought that to be beyond my ability, I knew exactly what he meant by his advice. As a matter of fact, the international community led primarily by the US, started "bashing" Japan for providing insufficient support towards global causes. Nowadays, Japan is considered to be doing nothing, or close to it, in terms of its contribution to the global society.

The chairman was aware of this problem and through that conversation, gave me an important assignment in his unique manner, to find an effective solution to bring Japan back on track.

As we were enjoying our coffee, a news program came on the television broadcasting a debate in parliament over the issue of budget allocation for Japanese highway construction programs. The chairman uttered as he watched the news, "The future of Japan will remain unclear unless we start to look at our issues from an international standpoint from now on." I carelessly responded to his comment by saying," The Japanese government is not doing the job right." The chairman replied enthusiastically, "Why are you still counting on your government? If you don't like how the government handles the issue, you should solve it in your own way instead." I cannot stress more that the chairman was way beyond the rest of us in his thinking by being proactive instead of reactive. It was his dynamic way of thinking and aggressive attitude by nature that enabled him to successfully lead Toyota as the first president after the merger between the production and marketing departments, as well as assuming the most prestigious position as the chairman of Japanese Federation of Economic Organizations from 1994 to 1998.

As you may know, the honorable chairman, Dr. Shoichiro Toyoda, is the eldest son of the late Toyota founder, Mr. Kiichiro Toyoda and is a cousin to the supreme advisor, Mr. Eiji Toyoda, who is his senior by 12 years. These two examples illustrate the need to look beyond self-imposed constraints, even in areas beyond our day-to-day activities.

Setting High Standards

Report Directly to Me in a Case of Emergency

When I joined the sales and marketing department in 1964, the president of Toyota was the late Mr. Shotaro Kamiya. When Mr. Kamiya was a top executive of General Motors Asia Pacific Japan, he was offered a position by Mr. Kiichiro Toyoda to work for Toyota immediately after its establishment. His proven abilities and professionalism in sales and marketing brought success to Toyota. Therefore he was often referred to as the "Godfather of sales and marketing."

At present in Japan there are about 308 dealers and about 5,800 retail locations under those dealerships. About 290 out of the existing 308 dealerships are independently owned. This is one of the characteristics of Toyota's way in sales and marketing, as domestic sales in many other competitors are supported by the investment made by manufacturers themselves. It was Mr. Kamiya who expanded the networks of private investment dealerships throughout Japan and established the trusting relationships among them; this was based on the principle of co-existence and co-prosperity. Unfortunately, I did not have the honor to meet Mr. Kamiya in person. However,

Figure 55: Shotaro Kamiya, First President of Toyota Sales & Marketing Division

©Toyota Motor Corporation
Used with permission. Permission does not
imply endorsement.

I have had many opportunities to learn directly from Mr. Seishi Kato whom Mr. Kamiya had trusted as his right hand man since his career at GM.

During my second year working in the overseas operations, Mr. Kato became the executive vice-president at the headquarters office after having finished his role as the president for the dealership located in Osaka. I did not expect Mr. Kato to pay any attention to someone like myself given the fact that I was only a junior employee with the company for two years. However, he immediately memorized my name and told me, "Make sure you report directly to me in case of an emergency. You do not need permission from your supervisor. I will phone you and do the same to you." To my surprise, he actually called me on many occasions and told me, "This is Kato. Please come see me right away. I need your help." He was quite particular about how each duty was performed, at the same time he urged us to solve problems as quickly as possible. When we were having a hard time reaching a consensus between the production and marketing divisions due to differences of opinion, he criticized us saying, "What is taking you so long to draw a conclusion? Just finish it right now!"

Sometimes, he was an extremely intimidating individual to many fresh faces like mine. However, the most significant lesson that I learned from Mr. Kato, who was open-minded yet demanded prompt answers from his employees, was to improve the flow in our work environment so that we can make accurate decisions in a timely manner.

Seishi Kato's Lessons Tested Workers' Flexibility in Problem Solving

When I was serving as an expatriate executive in Australia, I received some special training from Mr. Kato, who was already being promoted as the president of Toyota Motor Sales Co., Ltd. at the time. At one point he came to Sydney to attend a dinner party with representatives from Australian distributors. He gave me an order before the dinner by telling me, "I am going to give an introduction speech in Japanese, so, translate my speech into English for everyone else." I figured that his speech would not be too long to translate on the spot and replied casually by saying, "I will be glad to be of service." I did not have a notebook to take notes for translating his words, but I thought that writing on a napkin would be sufficient.

Mr. Kato stood up and started giving his speech without stopping to give me a chance to translate. I kept taking down my notes on a napkin only to find out that I was running out of room to write. His wife saw me struggling and whispered into his ear, "Honey, if you don't break up your speech, how is Yoshi going to translate for you?" Mr. Kato simply ignored his wife's advice and continued his speech without leaving any breaks. Party guests were observing me in somewhat of a panic with a grin on their faces and appeared quite interested in how I was going to translate all of his speech at once. He finally finished his speech and it was my turn to translate. Even though I felt that I was having cold sweats, I managed to complete the task at hand. His wife gave me a great compliment by saying "What a great translation. I am very impressed with your ability." However, Mr. Kato pretended as if nothing had happened and did not care

Figure 56: Seishi Kato

©Toyota Motor Corporation
Used with permission. Permission does not imply endorsement.

how I performed. He basically put me to the test and the way he did it was far better than any other method of teaching. He tested my English ability by giving me a long speech to translate on the spot. I admit that it was a harsh way, but his way was probably the most effective way to find out for certain.

Another example of Mr. Kato's unique teaching method was when he changed his busy schedule and came back to Sydney to attend the distributors' convention for the Metropolitan region. When we were about to eat lunch, he asked me out of the blue to write his speech in English from scratch. As we were under a tight schedule, my plan was to leave for the convention from the guest dining room right after finishing coffee. That meant there was not much time for me to prepare a speech. I snuck out of the dining room when Mr. Kato was enjoying his coffee and hurried back into my office. With the help from my Australian secretary, I wrote up a draft of his speech in 10 minutes. As I was driving Mr. Kato to the convention and we were about half way to our destination, he asked me, "By the way, do you have my speech written out yet?" I took out a neatly typed speech out of my pocket and handed it to him. He received it by simply saying, "This will do." Later as I heard him give the speech, I discovered that he made some corrections as he spoke. For example, he changed my sentence, "I arrived in Sydney from Jakarta this morning," to "Having arrived from Jakarta this morning."

As illustrated by my experiences, Mr. Kato occasionally tested my English to see if any improvements had been made and evaluated my flexibility in dealing with difficult problems or emergency situations. There was a deep-rooted purpose in his lessons by reminding his workers of the importance of maintaining a sense of urgency at all times.

Mindset of Expatriate Executives

As I continued to receive surprise tests from Mr. Kato, I began to think of a way to surprise him in return. I made advanced arrangements for many plans with different scenarios for accommodating Mr. Kato when he returned to Australia. This was because he did not like wasting his time. Upon arrival, I often asked him, "So, what would you like to see on this trip: dealerships or component warehouses?" Then, he chose visiting some component warehouses, at which point it would have been too late to make the necessary arrangements. Therefore, I held meetings with staff from both the dealerships and component warehouses in advance so that all of the essential preparations could be made for whatever Mr. Kato decided to do on a particular day. When we arrived at the component warehouse, Mr. Kato was surprised to see the Japanese flag accompanied by a banner that read, "Welcome, Mr. Seishi Kato!" He also enjoyed the reception table we had prepared for his arrival. He looked quite satisfied with this treatment and must have thought highly of our hospitality even though we were not told exactly where he was planning to visit.

Ever since this event, I made sure to continue arranging different plans for each visit that Mr. Kato made. I would brainstorm all day for ideas by which I could impress him even more by predicting his agenda for a specific trip. I even arranged separate plans to be used for sunny days or rainy days as well as plans for entertaining his wife if she decided to come along.

I can tell you from my experience of having been an expatriate executive for many years, it is always challenging to find out what the top executives are expecting to observe when they visit. We need to make sure that each top executive is given an opportunity to absorb as much local information as possible in every situation.

I strongly believe that expatriate executive officers must learn about the local community and constantly develop better plans for their visitors with a mindset that they can be committed to working around the clock. I want to emphasize here to avoid any misunderstandings about Mr. Kato. He is an innately kind and friendly person even though he is always strict about work. Since my very first assignment was to be the person in charge of Korea, Mr. Kato casually greeted me by jokingly saying, "Hey, Mr. Korea!" and continued to call me the same even after I moved on to Australia and the US regions. I tried to correct him many times by saying, "Mr. Kato, I am not in charge of Korea anymore," but, he always replied to me with a smile on his face, "It's not a big deal. You were in charge of Korea once, so you might as well be Mr. Korea."

The spirit of "3Cs for Harmonious Growth" was a corporate slogan developed by Mr. Kato when he became the president of Toyota Motor Sales Co., Ltd. No matter how harsh his assignments seemed to be, he was teaching me important lessons, I always loved his true personality that cherished the principles of, *Communication, Consideration,* and *Cooperation.*

Hiroshi Okuda is Always Right

Figure 57: Hiroshi Okuda the 8th President of Toyota

©Toyota Motor Corporation
Used with permission. Permission does not imply endorsement.

The first hybrid technology vehicle, "Prius," celebrated its 10th Anniversary after its release into the consumer market. Prius can run either by an electric motor or gasoline engine and has a remarkably high fuel efficiency of 35.5km per liter. Sales of Prius have increased in recent years due to the rise in the price of gasoline, and Toyota's effort towards protecting the environment has become a more evident factor. Honestly speaking, I was skeptical that Prius could produce legitimate and profitable business for Toyota 10 years ago. I am sure that I was not the only one with the concern. Not only Toyota's employees, but also experts in the industry, had negative views towards the unclear future of Prius as a hybrid vehicle.

This was because of the fact that the production of a hybrid system mounted on a Prius was estimated to cost about 300,000 Yen (approximately $3,000, U.S.) more than that of a conventional gasoline engine vehicle. Our challenge was to persuade customers that the additional costs could justify the true advantages of the Prius. As a matter of fact, a consumer survey once asked people a question, "How much more comfortable do you

146

feel in spending to purchase a hybrid vehicle?" The most typical answer was, "As high as 200,000 Yen." At that point, we already knew that there was a substantial difference of about 100,000 Yen between how much consumers were willing to pay and the actual cost of production.

However, the president at the time, Mr. Hiroshi Okuda, had a completely different perspective. He made his decision telling all of us that, "The economy will become much more conscious towards the environment in the 21st century. Therefore, I foresee a considerable demand for fuel-efficient vehicles from now on. Toyota must jump on it and lead the industry."

His decision triggered the production and marketing of the Prius line after having overcome the initial criticism from those who thought that it was just too soon. Mr. Okuda's final decision is also considered to be as courageous and influential as the decision made by Mr. Eiji Toyoda for establishing the Lexus brand in the past. Consequently, Prius alone had sold more than one million vehicles by April of 2008.

The spirit of Toyota is clearly represented by the successful examples of Lexus and Prius. Toyota is essentially a collective team with its solid foundation of, "3Cs for Harmonious Growth" (*Constant, Consistent* and *Continuous*) and "3Cs for Innovation" (*Creativity, Challenge* and *Courage*) and is never afraid of exploring outside of the norms and of its comfort zone as long as Toyota continues to sustain itself in its deep rooted philosophy.

Mr. Okuda made the right decision by confronting what needed to be addressed. As demonstrated in the Prius case, by verbalizing the reasoning behind his decisions, his approach makes perfect sense in any set of circumstances. He was extremely active in expanding Toyota globally and much of Toyota's success in the international market can be attributed to his dedication.

Personally, he was one of the most influential superiors I ever had. At the same time, as I finished my expatriate duty in Australia and returned to Japan, Mr. Okuda, after having completed his expatriate role in the Philippines, also returned to Japan to become the general manager of the Asia and Oceania department. This is when I began working under his direct supervision. Mr. Okuda mentored me because we both started our careers in the sales and marketing division and we were graduates of the same university. He taught me many important things in professional settings as well as the necessary business mannerisms in social settings. He is into playing mahjong games and singing karaoke. He loves reading books and has a great appreciation for many different genres of movies. When we talked about work, he was always able to give me only the right answers in the most logical manner, which often made me realize that I had a long way to go as a professional. Even more amazing, no matter how late we were drinking, Mr. Okuda was never late or absent the next day. His vitality is stronger than anyone I know, and I have a great deal of respect for him simply for who he is. After fulfilling the role of the chairman for Japan Federation of Economic Organization, Mr. Okuda now serves as the special advisor to the Japanese Cabinet, which proves that he has become a strong leader not only within Toyota, but also in a territory beyond the framework of Toyota.

Learning from a Business Management Scholar, Ikujiro Nonaka

The list of individuals who have influenced me the most cannot be complete without mentioning professor Ikujiro Nonaka. Even though he was not a Toyota employee, his name is well-known as a business management scholar. Mr. Nonaka, is an honorary professor at Hitotsubashi University and a special emeritus professor in the department of Xerox knowledge at the graduate college of business management at the University of California, Berkeley. More recently, he is a First Distinguished Drucker Scholar, at the Drucker School, Claremount Graduate

University, in California. He is widely known as the creator of the theory of "Knowledge Management." However, I discovered him through one of his books entitled, *Essence of Failure*, which describes reasons why the Japanese military was defeated so badly in the Pacific War by presenting a series of his organizational theories. I was extremely impressed with the book and praised it to be an extremely valuable asset for learning about critical business management principles.

I had a great opportunity to meet Mr. Nonaka in person through our mutual colleague at Hitotsubashi University. I discovered by accident that he had been teaching courses at the Graduate School of International Corporate Strategy (ICS). I contacted Professor Takeuchi, who was in charge of coordinating academic research collaboration between Toyota and the University, to introduce me to Mr. Nonaka. What impressed me the most in my discussions with him, and reading a number of his publications, was the expression "dialectic approach." We often said to one another in Toyota, "Do not give up because it is impossible. Focus on the neutralizing aspect of the contradiction-causing factors at a higher level of dimension."

Figure 58: Ikujiro Nonaka

Mr. Nonaka taught me that the dialectic approach was representing the same philosophy within our corporate philosophies such as:

- Stay global with a locally-oriented mind (Glocal).

- Seek the ultimate efficiency, yet respect human nature.

- Produce advanced vehicles by reducing costs.

- Design high performance vehicles that are environmentally sound.

Each contains seemingly contradicting factors. However, do not allow them to conflict with one another. Find a way to bring them into harmony on the most sophisticated level. Toyota has been doing exactly that for a long time and I can now classify Toyota's methods as a dialectic approach.

Mr. Nonaka also taught me the importance of "openness." Management executives must continue to create opportunities where different ideas are openly discussed in order to build common values within their teams. There are many companies wishing to implement the Toyota Way into their operations. However, it is not an easy thing to do. In many cases, business owners leave the entire implementation process to consultants only to suffer from a superficial result at the end. The answer is neither to give direct orders from upper management, nor to strictly follow corporate practices designed to train employees. The answer is to unite upper management and the shop floor workers and create an environment for open discussion and formulate solutions to make our ideal goals tangible, instead of shifting away from our tendency to conclude arguments with an "all or nothing" method.

I also learned a valuable lesson from Mr. Nonaka's recent book titled, *Virtuous-Based Management*. The book mainly talks about how business schools in the US and universities in Japan excessively teach their students only "How to" but they should focus more on teaching the fundamental philosophies behind

becoming a successful business person instead. It also emphasizes the importance of business leaders maintaining practical
knowledge-based leadership. I could go on and on describing
this book since I am a big fan. However, I will just recommend
it for you to read this book yourself so I will not give away too
many secrets here.

CHAPTER 7

FUTURE THREATS

"Corporate Disease" is the Most Intimidating Thing

As I continue to learn from the wisdom of Mr. Nonaka, I often question myself, "What does Toyota need the most from now on?" In fact, I am most afraid of "corporate disease." It is the adverse effect of companies growing too large in size, and has the potential to pose serious risks that are negatively related to:

- Inability to coordinate efforts within the company

- Lack of true leadership

- Weakened spirit to challenge new things

More importantly, the most critical factor, which we need to pay our closest attention to, is how to retain the sense of risk awareness within the company.

Until now, Toyota has taught every single employee to always be aware of risks, which was the main reason for Toyota's continuous advancement. No matter how greatly Toyota's profits were increasing, Toyota always predicted and was prepared for the risks that were hidden in its path into the future. By asking questions such as:

"What if we lose to competition in ten years?"

"What if our revenues go down due to the increasing value of the Japanese Yen?"

"What happens to Toyota if a catastrophic natural disaster occurs at some point in the future?"

Toyota has learned from the actual risks in the past and developed unique techniques to minimize the impact of such crises.

When a serious earthquake struck the Niigata prefecture in July of 2007, Riken Corporation, which is a well-known supplier in the auto industry, was forced to stop its operation and caused serious setbacks on the production of Japanese domestic automakers. Riken Corporation is the largest independent company that manufactures one of the most important auto components, engine piston rings, and maintains a domestic share of 50%. If Riken's factories stop their productions for some reason, it means that domestic automakers have to stop their production as well.

When the earthquake struck the Riken factory, auto-makers—including Toyota—immediately sent emergency units to the location and provided recovery support in any way they could in order to put Riken's production back on track. From this event, we as automakers, learned an important lesson. We became aware from that situation, in which the stoppages from the Riken's factory could terminate the entire business operation of the domestic automakers, had to be reexamined. In my opinion, there had to be many solutions to this problem such as negotiating with Riken officials to build a secondary factory in a different location or to share their techniques and knowledge so that other auto suppliers could develop new production capabilities and reallocation to other suppliers. In cases like this where a serious inconvenience was experienced, we must not only develop solutions in a timely manner, but also formulate preventive policies at a fundamental level in order to effectively handle similar issues in the future. This is truly what it means to have a sense of risk awareness.

Fuel Efficiency of the Next Generation Hybrid Vehicles

One of Toyota's biggest challenges in the future is how to effectively service highly computerized vehicles from now on. Around the year 2000, Mercedes discovered various defects that were caused by computer bugs in their vehicles and received a tremendous amount of customer complaints, which eventually affected their sales for more than two years.

Toyota has also had to deal with an increased number of recalls caused by computer glitches. These glitches are extremely difficult to detect, even under the extensive quality control processes. For example, where would you take your car to replace your battery for a new one? I assume that most of you take it to a nearby gas station or an independent car mechanic. It was perfectly fine to do this in the past. However, technologically advanced modern cars, especially luxury cars, the process is more extensive when replacing a battery. Usually when replacing something as common as a battery, four different processes of computer initialization have to be performed using advanced equipment, otherwise these cars may end up with some serious defects. Dysfunctional automatically adjustable rear-view mirrors and inaccurate indication of the warning lights, even when all the doors are properly shut, can result. Legitimate dealerships do not experience such problems as they have the specialized equipment provided by Toyota. However, places like gas stations in general fail to provide the same services due to the lack of the necessary equipment, as well as the lack of properly trained mechanics which will most likely increase the potential for producing more problems in Toyota cars. I know that choosing the right place to obtain appropriate services can cause a great level of inconvenience to our customers. How we make this process easier and comprehensive is one of the biggest challenges for all of the existing automakers today to solve.

Another challenge, of course, is for automakers to extend their efforts to mitigate various environmental issues. Toyota plans to introduce new hybrid models for both the Lexus and Toyota product lines at the International Auto Show that will take place in North America in 2009. Toyota also is planning to sell to the global market, mainly in the US, the "Plug-in Hybrid Vehicle" that can be recharged by any household electric outlets and has twice the fuel efficiency as the existing Prius models.

Figure 59: Prius Plug–In Hybrid

©Toyota Motor Corporation
Used with permission. Permission does not
imply endorsement.

Each of these examples demonstrates the mixed blessings of new technology. It also shows the challenge, when existing consumer practices must change; and, how consumer behavior patterns are difficult to influence.

How We React to Decreased Consumer Interest in Owning an Automobile

Japan's domestic sales of new automobiles have not been impressive in recent years. The changing demographics such as the serious societal phenomena of fewer children and aging of the population are such factors. Some researchers blame the plunging of auto sales on the young generations who choose not to own an automobile in order to avoid getting stuck in traffic jams and the high costs of parking, particularly in the urban areas. As vehicles last longer, more people are keeping their cars longer. In order to battle this problem, we need to reinforce our used-car sales operation for providing affordable prices and establish comprehensive post-sales services for recruiting hesitant new car buyers in order to keep our revenues flowing. Even Toyota is developing a number of so-called "Wellcab" vehicles for handicapped people and aging generations to help ease their mobility.

I do not mean that Toyota has given up on making our cars appealing to younger generations. Toyota strongly believes that younger generations can become our loyal customers throughout their lives. We can do this with automobiles that attract their attention with our entry-level cars and by giving them the opportunity to experience the proven quality of our cars combined with respectful customer care. As a matter of fact, Toyota introduced its sub-brand called "Scion" in the USA, which began targeting the younger generations in their 20s, also referred to as "Generation Y," in 2003. The brand, "Scion" belongs to neither mass-consumer, nor luxury car categories. It has been extremely successful and is a good example of Toyota's creating a whole new brand category to be marketed to a specific niche of consumers.

The Japanese market will continue to be segmented due to

Figure 60: The Toyota Scion

©Toyota Motor Corporation
Used with permission. Permission does not
imply endorsement.

the aging of the domestic population. It can be an extremely rewarding business experience if we continue being responsive to society's needs, such as developing user-friendly vehicles not only for younger generations but also for middle-aged and elderly consumers. A number of households in the countryside own two or three cars. The main transportation method in the countryside is by far the automobile. Therefore, families have to utilize a number of cars with various specifications and features to serve their specific purposes. One usage may be for performing some field work on a farm, for grandparents to run small errands in town, and for sons to commute to their work on a daily basis. In addition, rural roads are narrow and hard to navigate. There is strong demand for cars with the highest level of safety in these areas, especially for elderly drivers. I am talking about accident-proof cars that can be used for both doing farm work and commuting at little expense in the sense of luxury and capability of running at a high speed. I believe there must be many innovative ideas to create such cars, such as installing more sensors for automatic braking mechanisms, and improving the visibility of the instrument gauges. Wisdom is infinity.

Improving the Functionality of Automobile Sales Financing

In general, automobile sales and marketing functions are closely connected with automobile sales financing. Originally, the growth of the automobile industry is contributed to the development of various finance programs. Traditionally speaking,

158

the most popular method of payment was for customers to remit monthly installments, especially for purchasing expensive items. In recent years, loans and credit card payments are the most common practice among consumers, for which automakers have been developing flexible and affordable financing plans in order to accommodate unique financial needs of their customers.

Automobile sales financing can be classified into two categories. One category being the financing plans called "Floor Plan Financing," which is designed to help dealerships acquire dealer inventory, in other words, a wholesale finance system. Dealerships are usually required to sign a payment contract to be paid off within a two month-period when they are supplied with a new stock.

The other category called "Retail Financing," is designed to finance consumers who are purchasing items from dealerships. Customers will take over the loan for the items from the dealership and are generally required to pay it off within 36 or 48 month periods. Customers usually submit a down payment that is 20% of the total value and pay the remaining 80% in any way they feel financially comfortable within a given time frame.

Most of Toyota's customers tend to go with three- or four-year loans. Nowadays, Toyota has also been providing customers with various other payment options by establishing Toyota's own captive finance companies so that every specific financial situation of each customer can be well taken care of. For example, Toyota exclusively offers "Leasing Plans," which allows customers to submit much lower monthly payments for a certain percentage of the total loan amount. At the end of their payment plan, they are given options of paying off the remaining balance or sell their cars back to dealerships in order to exchange for a new vehicle. This program has been extremely popular as it allows customers much flexibility and a potential to own luxury cars that they would have not been able to afford otherwise.

There are many other considerate financing programs that can be used to purchase Toyota cars, such as: plans that offers financing and auto insurance simultaneously (Combination Plan), plans that allow consumer to adjust their monthly payments according to the changes in their lifestyles (Adjustable Rate Plan), and plans designed for seniors allowing them to pay with their social security benefits on a bimonthly basis.

Consumers' purchasing methods for automobiles

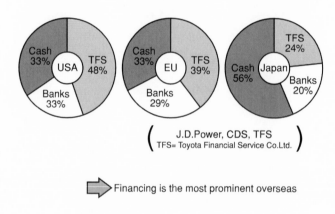

$$\left(\begin{array}{c} \text{J.D.Power, CDS, TFS} \\ \text{TFS= Toyota Financial Service Co.Ltd.} \end{array} \right)$$

Financing is the most prominent overseas

Figure 61: Large Market Auto Finance Options

Toyota has been setting up a system called, "One-stop Service" with great success at dealerships throughout Japan, where customers can compare all of the available financing options and apply for the most suitable one just by visiting a dealership. However, the problem as I indicated in the figure, is that business transactions in Japan are still cash-based compared to the US and European markets, therefore the effectiveness of these innovative financing programs we have in Japan is yet to be proven to be fully functional and as effective as we expect it can be. There is no doubt that Toyota still has a long way to go in their future to fully implement these financing programs in order to be more successful in sales and marketing.

Aggravated Competition in the BRICs Market

Tata Motors belongs to an Indian financial group called the "Tata Group." Tata Motors introduced at the New Delhi Auto Expo in January of 2008, a series of light automobile models called "Nano" with a price tag of only about 280,000 Yen ($2,800 US). Nano announced that they will start selling in India as

Figure 62: The Tata "Nano"

early as the fall of 2008 and is bound to seriously raise the competition among automakers in producing affordable cars that are primarily targeted to the BRICs marketing regions consisting of Brazil, Russia, India, China and third world countries. In fact, in 2007, Toyota sold about 500,000 cars in the Chinese market, second only to the US market in the numbers of cars sold in a foreign country. It is expected that 750,000 cars are to sell in 2008 and the sales will reach the 1,000,000 barrier in the next few years. As these markets grow, so does their importance.

For a long time, Toyota was clearly aware that the Chinese market would soon grow as large as the US market. Toyota exported the "Crown" model to China in 1964 and began production on Chinese soil in 2002, after having initiated the technical collaboration agreement with First Automobile Works Group in 1978. The production is carried out by the amalgamated corporation between First Automobile Works Group in Northern China and GAC (Guanghzou Toyota) in Southern China, splitting in each venture a 50-50 partnership.

As for the Russian Market, Toyota is expanding its marketing territory rather aggressively compared to how Toyota has always been advancing into a new foreign country. Russia is a country whose politics are quite implicitly represented by the Northern Territory Issues, which poses a great deal of risk to foreign companies for conducting business on Russian soil. In spite of these uncertainties, Toyota foresaw a growing demand in the Russian market and began the production of Camry models in December of 2007, at the rate of 20,000 cars per year at the main factory located in St. Petersburg, Russia. Toyota's marketing networks have already expanded from Moscow to the Yekaterinburg region, which is located near the borders to Asia, along the Ural mountain ranges. The total number of cars sold in 2006 for the entire Russian region easily exceeded 160,000 cars.

Toyota's "Instant Full Recovery" and "Pre-Service"

Marketing experts like me have always strongly emphasized the importance of the "after-sales service." Needless to say, the after-sales service is a series of services that we provide after customers have purchased their cars. As we have been providing various services such as repairs, procurement of the necessary components, and providing maintenance notifications to customers, these services are now taken for granted and are referred as the "pre-service."

Our conventional method was to create repair manuals after the completion of a car and the repair manuals were distributed to the dealerships for their mechanics to be trained on repairs and maintenance. However, this method can actually lead to inconvenience for providing services. The challenge is to anticipate problems before they occur, especially problems related to poor product design. For example, say, the designer decides to shorten the length of the oil dipstick to save some production costs and places the oil level gauge near the back of the engine to compensate for the shorter reach of the dip stick. This is a kind of idea that pays no consideration to service technicians. Changing the location of the oil level gauge made it difficult for the technician to reach while the engine is hot.

In order to avoid this kind of inconvenience a new system is in place where service technicians can get involved in the designing process and make a suggestion like, "Please place the oil level gauge on the front side of the engine for much easier access." This entire process is called "Design-In" that incorporates ideas from various experts other than designers in development of new vehicles. In other words, this is what we call the "pre-service," which is designed to provide solutions at a very early stage of design for making the "after-sales services" performed much easier and error-free.

As for the "after-sales services," Toyota has never failed to maintain the full-blown operations of customer care. Toyota sent excellent service technicians to 12 different locations throughout Japan and built a strong network of skills and knowledge, which allowed Toyota to provide a "fix it right the first time" treatment to every single problem around the world. "Fix it right the first time" means that every problem must be identified and eliminated after one comprehensive repair in order to avoid reoccurring defects without any identifiable causes.

In order to provide a "fix it right the first time" service to our customers, training of highly skilled engineers is absolutely necessary. Toyota's service training institute located in Nisshin of Aichi Prefecture administrates specialized training courses based on Toyota's unique certification programs in order to educate mechanics at dealerships. Toyota's training has built-in mechanisms that teach its mechanics the most advanced and up-to-date techniques while at the same time improving the quality of the diagnostic courses. These courses prepare mechanics for working with complex and computerized components and they adjust the curriculum annually, according to changes in technology.

Although Toyota's mechanics are taught the operational standard of, "Toyota dealerships must complete a comprehensive maintenance inspection within one hour," they are also required to learn how to maintain various dealership facilities and tools used in the service center, as well as establish standardized service manuals for their team to follow. Training for Toyota mechanics includes preparing for an ideal work environment, in which appropriate diagnostic analysis can be carried out by utilizing the intranet information system to retrieve the essential service information. Training also teaches mechanics how to implement a system in which the most efficient way of completing the necessary operations can be shared among other mechanics by creating their original movie tutorials and written manuals. By progressing these techniques and skills of Toyota mechanics, with attention to detail, and improving overall work efficiency, Toyota continues to reinforce the activity of providing an effective "fix it right the first time" service.

These various examples show the complexity of issues which must be considered by manufacturers. Improved technology, the need to meet ecological concerns and energy conservation, changing demographics, changing societal values, emerging markets, and the list goes on, show the need for innovation and productivity improvements in the whole supply chain. These present leadership with a challenge to avoid corporate diseases and hardening of the arteries. Nimbleness, staying in tune with the markets, and willingness to face reality are a must.

Summary

As I have presented you various explanations of the Toyota Way and Toyota Way in Sales and Marketing, I strongly urge you to ask yourself the following question,

"What aspects of the Toyota Way and Toyota Way in Sales Marketing should you focus on in order to effectively apply the new knowledge to other types of businesses in the future?"

In my opinion, we must go back to the basics and put an

emphasis on analyzing the existing organizational cultures as well as the environment in which such a culture is being created. Providing opportunities to inspire open communication among workers and promoting desirable corporate cultures are indispensable for sharing common values so that many difficult challenges can be overcome in a most effective manner. Management leaders must take steps towards establishing such an appropriate corporate culture and make every effort to introduce a mechanism for sharing mutual values among his workers ,who are responsible for performing each departmental duty. Active participation from each organizational member must be called for and, most importantly, the implementation of "Visualization" must be prioritized for an organization to initiate sharing of its common values internally. As the 21st century has dramatically flourished due to information technology, it is equally important for organizations to adopt a proven mechanism of Information Technology, which helps organizations achieve their goals in the long run with a great deal of certainty.

I cannot stress more that the goal of implementing "Visualization" within management operations does not end with simply bringing critical information to the surface. We must understand that the true objective of "Visualization" enables management to effectively embed the true implication of the organization's collective goals among every single staff member at all levels of the organization.

Toyota has always focused on achieving "Visualization" of information by creating opportunities for open communications. Consequently, it is encouraged that Toyota's common values identified by "Visualization" be utilized for conducting benchmark analysis against other problematic areas. In Toyota's terminologies, this process is called "Yokoten," meaning that commonly shared values are being applied horizontally to influence the same outcome outside your boundary.

Today, we are exposed to an overwhelming amount of information that comes from a variety of media. It is the result of the substantial leap in the field of Information Technology. As available information continues to flood us all, it is human intelligence that enables us to select only the useful information and apply it to bring about our own betterment. As for corporate environment, it is true to say that symptoms of detrimental information often remain unnoticed for the lack of "Visualization" in many organizational settings. As you already know, this never leads to any improvement in your strength of management. What is demanded here is creating an environment in which negative information and undesirable tendencies can be constantly addressed at freewill by "Visualization." The Toyota Way becomes ingrained in your organization's DNA only when management establishes a desirable corporate culture where each shop floor worker is entitled to actively engage in disclosing issues in the most honest manner.

As your organization continues to swell in size, "Yokoten" becomes more challenging. Critical information that has become apparent through "Visualization" becomes lost by the walls created by the increased volume of information. In order to eliminate such a consequence, Toyota has been practicing what is known as "Obeya (which simply means "big room" in Japanese) Activity," which helps Toyota carry out internal cross-departmental projects more efficiently. Project leaders as well as members of the organization assemble into the Obeya and develop clearer understandings for each process within a project or the project itself by sharing information that became apparent through Visualization. Such information is posted on the walls in Obeya for participants to capture comprehensive views on a given project as well. In my opinion, there is clearly no argument that this unique collective process functions as an effective tool for preventing an adverse corporate disease to occur in the first place. In addition, Toyota coordinates an organization called "Business Reform" for a limited time to perform as a Cross Functional Team, which is designed to eliminate sectionalism among departments within the company. I believe that Toyota has been able to derive a great deal of positive results from this technique as well.

It is human intelligence that enables us to create such a remarkable organizational structure and effectively administer it. As well, it is our individual strengths that can manipulate such an organizational structure in order to accomplish continuous improvements for daily activities of our corporation. It is the intelligence of Toyota's forerunners that transplanted human elements in machinery (Jidoka — Automation with a Human Touch), allowing the underlying issues on the shop floor to be easily identified by every single worker. Utilizing the power of human intelligence to its full potential and repeating continuous improvement on the shop floor is our never-ending challenge. In other words, I would like to conclude this book by saying that human intelligence is infinite and continuous improvement is eternal.

AFTERWORD

The financial catastrophe caused by the sub-prime loan crisis in the United States has spread rapidly beyond its borders and subsequently led to a severe global economic recession. In the summer of 2008, people all over the world were intoxicated by the Beijing Olympics where athletes across the globe continued to set new world records. At the same time, the price of crude oil jumped up to as high as $150 per barrel, which sky-rocketed the cost of transporting various raw materials to what we refer to as the "Factory of the World," China. The increase in oil price also significantly influenced not only the price of essential food, but also risked the distribution of provisions across the world.

Who on earth could ever have predicted that a global crisis of this magnitude could strike us so sharply, especially in the early part of year 2008? Many experts are categorizing this crisis as a worldwide depression that usually occurs once in every hundred years. Experts continue to publish various editorial comments for the purpose of explaining this phenomenon by reflecting upon the series of events that had occurred during the world economic depression of 1929.

General Motors celebrated its 100th anniversary in September of 2008 and announced their strong determination to remain king of the automakers for the next one hundred years. However, in reality, General Motor was suffering from a significant decrease in market demand for their large pickup trucks and utility vehicles. As for the entire US market, annual sales have dropped from 16 million plus cars per year to just 12 million.

GMAC Financial Services was left no choice but to conduct selective financing due to this global financial contraction. GMAC also failed to resource adequate financial investment to meet the future sales goals of General Motors, as the trust in General Motors has significantly diminished among investors. It was indeed an unimaginable change that nobody had ever expected to bring upon the entire automobile industry.

When I went on a business trip to Australia last October, I was extremely surprised to discover that GMAC had announced to plans to pull back their Australian operations entirely. I am pretty sure that readers of this book are already aware of this confusion imposed upon the US automakers and have been watching closely the whole process of US automakers struggling to receive emergency financial bailouts from the US federal government.

At any rate, the survival of the Detroit Three—General Motors, Ford, and Chrysler—is heavily dependent on their ability to overcome this current financial hardship while confronting various other challenges in the process. Not to mention that the fate of other automobile makers and component suppliers—as well as auto retailers across the US—are equally at stake and their fortunes are heavily dependent upon their outcome.

The magnitude of the present financial crisis is unparalleled in our history, as it attacked our economy both globally and simultaneously across the world. When critiqued by a perspective of light and dark, it is not an exaggeration to state that the effects of the global economy are casting the giant shadow of globalization as we speak. We have only gone through the entrance of a long dark tunnel, where we are most likely to encounter a random series of bends on our way out. However, I strongly believe that effective solutions to break out of this labyrinth can be discovered no matter how much time and effort are required.

Particularly during a crisis such as this, I become painfully aware that we must assess our way of work by revisiting the fundamental principles of the Toyota Way, which teaches us once again the strategies and solutions that are formulated by our predecessors in order to battle similar situations. I am confident that various innovative business models will be developed in the near future with an accumulation of our new ideas and continuous improvement.

As for the automobile manufactures of the future, they will concentrate their efforts on establishing a product line that consists of vehicles with much higher levels of safety, performance, and mobility, and by designing smaller passenger and commercial vehicles that are environmentally sound and run with high fuel efficiency.

More and more models of hybrid and fully-electric cars will be introduced to the global automobile market, eventually exceeding the number of gasoline and diesel cars on which our society has been heavily dependent. There is also a much greater chance for utilizing renewable resources such as solar energy in order for us to battle a possible energy crisis and help to eliminate various environmental issues.

I have been obsessed with automobiles since I was a child. As a college student, besides majoring in corporate law, I belonged to the automobile club with a tremendous amount of enthusiasm inside me. I decided to set my own goal to work for Toyota after I graduated. At the time Toyota was still divided into the production and marketing divisions. However, I did not hesitate to strongly request to be recruited into the sales division as I believed that I would be able to travel all around the world someday, once Japanese cars became popular in the global market.

I am talking about what I was going through more than 45 years ago. When I was 23 years old, I remember having big dreams and focusing on Toyota as a company. Never had I imagined that Toyota would become as successful as it is now. Needless to say, I never expected to serve in such honorable positions as the president of Toyota Motor Sales, U.S.A., Inc., and the executive vice-president of Toyota headquarters in Japan. I sometimes feel as though I was just dreaming about the whole thing.

My own great senior advisor Mr. Seishi Kato, whom I truly respect and admire always said, "The road to successful marketing is to maintain sincerity." What does it really mean to be "sincere?" This is how I always understood it:

"Sincerity" is to:

Put your ideas into action,

Do what needs to be done at all times,

Carry out what you already know is right.

It is basically all about how you conduct yourself in your own actions. I strongly believe that being sincere is to express yourself in a format that everyone else can easily understand or relate to. The spirit of sincerity within Toyota, also known as the Toyota Way, reveals its true meaning only when it is put into action. This principle can be applied to the Toyota Way in Sales and Marketing as well. Each employee must continue to fulfill his or her purposes on a daily basis for the purpose of achieving the true effectiveness of Toyota's goals.

What I have observed in the last 45 years of my career was essentially a collaboration of different actions performed by every single Toyota employee. In other words, it is a lifetime accumulation of Toyota's sincerity. No matter how each Toyota employee's actions may have varied in the level of dedication and led to either successful or unsuccessful results, every effort Toyota employees made was absolutely necessary to move ourselves forward one step at a time, towards realizing Toyota's ultimate ideals with a great confidence.

I hope that this book, designed to describe the Toyota Way in Sales and Marketing, explains the accumulation of Toyota's actions and provides value to all of you in one way or another. As I repeatedly emphasized in the book, the Toyota Way in Sales and Marketing consists of principles of actions and not of written manuals. The Toyota Way in Sales and Marketing is how Toyota employees stand on the fundamental principles and challenge themselves in flexible manners by incorporating their own intelligence and ideas into effective solutions.

I will be greatly honored to learn that you were able to benefit from Toyota's knowledge, as defined in this book, and received some useful guidance for your own pursuit of "My Way."

I would like to specially thank Mr. Hiroyuki Yasuma, Managing Director of Ishida TAISEISHA Inc. for providing me with a useful guideline and carefully reviewing the English translation of my original text. I would also like to thank John Kramer, the Vice President of the Toyota Global Knowledge Center for his advice in publishing this book in English.

June, 2009

Yoshio Ishizaka

LIST OF FIGURES

INDEX

SYMBOLS

A

APEC— 135

Autobytel. *See* Category Killers

Automobile Culture

by region— 117–119

Automobile sales financing— 159

AutoNation. *See* Category Killers

Auto Trade Friction— 77

B

Be a good listener— 111, 113

Be a student for life— 134

Big Corporate Disease— 126

BMW— 80, 120

BRICs Market— 161

Bubble economy— 128

C

Category Killers— 131, 132

Challenge— 2

Champions— 49-51

Cho, Fujio— 12

Communication— 11, 12, 24, 28, 31, 55, 64

Friedman, Thomas— 75

G

Gas Guzzler Tax— 98

Gates, Bill

as target customer— 78

Genchi-genbutsu— xxii, 2, 4, 6, 38, 52, 55, 59, 129, 137, 138

General Motors— xxi, 8, 77, 140, 172, 173

GKC— xxii, 15, 16, 45, 46, 49, 50, 53

main objective of— 15

Global Knowledge Center. *See* GKC

Glocal— 55-8, 150

GMAC Financial Services— 172

I

Inclusive Leadership— 111

Initial investment in inventory— 87

J

J. D. Power and Associates— 82, 91

Jidoka— 11, 12, 168

Just-In-Time— 8, 11, 12, 19, 20, 88, 90

Publications from Enna

Enna provides companies with the foundation of knowledge and practical implementation ideas that will ensure your efforts to internalize process improvement. Reach your vision and mission with the expertise within these world-class texts. Call toll-free (866) 249-7348 or visit us on the web at www.enna.com to order or request our free product catalog.

Kaizen and the Art of Creative Thinking

Read the book that New York Times Best Selling author of *The Toyota Way*, Jeffrey Liker says, "will help you understand the deep thinking that underlies the real practice of TPS." Dr. Shigeo Shingo's Scientific Thinking Mechanism is the framework from which Toyota and hundreds of other companies have utilized to manage creative problem solving.

ISBN 978–1–897363–59–1 | 2007 | $59.40 | Item: **909**

Fundamental Principles of Lean Manufacturing

Dr. Shingo breaks each one down to their separate components for review and improvement methods. From the pro's and con's of the division of labor, to lot size, delays, transportation, inspections, layout design and efficiency, and everything in between; Dr. Shingo is there to guide the reader towards solutions that work. Dr. Shingo goes into great depth concerning coefficient of Design and Layout Design—a fantastic set of tools that every reader should learn and use.

ISBN 978–1–926537–07–8 | 2010 | $64.80 | Item: **921**

The Principles of Scientific Management

Read the American classic that inspired Shigeo Shingo! Frederick W. Taylor's *The Principles of Scientific Management*, was a mental revolution that spawned the very ideas of process improvement, equity and efficiency between workers and management, and the attainability of high production with low labor costs. As the basis of modern organizational efficiency, this instrumental book has motivated managers and engineers for almost 100 years.

ISBN 978–1–897363–89–8 | 2008 | $21.99| Item: **912**

The Strategos Guide to Value Stream & Process Mapping

The Strategos Guide to Value Stream and Process Mapping has proven strategies and helpful tips on facilitating group VSM exercises and puts VSM in the greater Lean context. With photos and examples of related Lean practices, the book focuses on implementing VSM, not just drawing diagrams and graphs.

ISBN 978–1–897363–43–0 | 2007 | $47.00 | Item: **905**

The Idea Generator, Quick and Easy Kaizen

The book discusses the Kaizen mind set that enables a company to utilize its resources to the fullest by directly involving all of its manpower in the enhancement and improvement of the productivity of its operations. Published and co–written by Norman Bodek, the *Godfather of Lean*.

ISBN 978–0971243699 | 2001 | $47.52 | Item: **902**

JIT is Flow

Hirano's *5 Pillars of the Visual Workplace* and *JIT Implementation Manual* were classics. They contained detailed descriptions of techniques and clear instructions. This book highlights the depth of the thought process behind Hirano's work. The clarity which Hirano brings to JIT/ Lean and the delineation of the principles involved will be invaluable to every leader and manager aiming for business excellence.

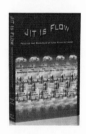

ISBN 978–0971243613 | 2006 | $47.52 | Item: **903**

Jit Factory Flow Kit

This hands–on simulation demonstrates the effectiveness of Just-in-Time compared to normal manufacturing; it shows how much easier job functions can be and how efficient all employees can become if the simple and easy rules of JIT are followed. It is dynamic enough for high–level management training, yet has enough detail for production staff; provides the "Ah–ha, I get it!" factor. In less than two hours you will have all your staff agreeing to move to a Lean System.

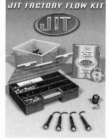

ISBN 978–1–897363–60–7 | 2007 | $479.99 | Item: **1081**

Study Mission to Japan

We are excited to present an exclusive trip to the birthplace of Lean. We provide a one-week unique tour at a reasonable all-inclusive price that will guide you to a better understanding of Lean Manufacturing principles. Enna has exclusive access to Toyota and Toyota suppliers due to our publications of Dr. Shigeo Shingo's classic manuscripts. You will have one-on-one access to Japanese Lean Executives and learn from their experiences and solutions. We also offer custom private tours for executive management teams over 12 people. Join us on our next tour by visiting www.enna.com/japantrip and register on-line or by telephone at: +1 (360) 306-5369

5S Training Package

Our 5S Solution Packages will help your company create a sustainable 5S program that will turn your shop floor around, and put you ahead of the competition. All of the benefits that come from Lean Manufacturing are built upon a strong foundation of 5S. Enna's solution packages will show you how to implement and sustain an environment of continuous improvement.
Version 1: ISBN 978–0–973750–90–4 | 2005 | $429.99 | Item: **12**
Version 2: ISBN 978–1–897363–25–6 | 2006 | $429.99 | Item: **17**
Version 1: Sort, Straighten, Sweep, Standardize, and Sustain
Version 2: Sort, Set In Order, Shine, Standardize, and Sustain

To Order: Phone, fax, email, or mail to Enna Products Corporation ATTN: Order Processing, 1602 Carolina Street, Unit B3, Bellingham, WA, 98229 USA. Phone: (866) 249-7348, Fax: (905) 481-0756, Email: info@enna.com. Send checks to this address. We accept all major credit cards. All prices are in US dollars and are subject to change without notice.